Study Guide

INFANT & CHILD

Study Guide

GARY BOTHE • SUSAN BOTHE
Pensacola Junior College

INFANT & CHILD

Development from Birth through Middle Childhood

JUDITH RICH HARRIS

ROBERT M. LIEBERT
State University of New York at Stony Brook

Prentice Hall, Englewood Cliffs, New Jersey 07632

Editorial production/supervision: *Geneviève Lopez*
Pre-press buyer: *Kelly Behr*
Manufacturing buyer: *Mary Ann Gloriande*
Supplement acquisitions editor: *Sharon Chambliss*
Acquisitions editor: *Carol Wada*

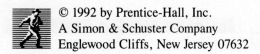

© 1992 by Prentice-Hall, Inc.
A Simon & Schuster Company
Englewood Cliffs, New Jersey 07632

Printed in the United States of America

10 9 8 7 6 5 4 3 2 1

ISBN 0-13-457714-0

Prentice-Hall International (UK) Limited, *London*
Prentice-Hall of Australia Pty. Limited, *Sydney*
Prentice-Hall Canada Inc., *Toronto*
Prentice-Hall Hispanoamericana, S.A., *Mexico*
Prentice-Hall of India Private Limited, *New Delhi*
Prentice-Hall of Japan, Inc., *Tokyo*
Simon & Schuster Asia Pte. Ltd., *Singapore*
Editora Prentice-Hall do Brasil, Ltda., *Rio de Janeiro*

Contents

READ THIS!
BEFORE YOU GO ANY FARTHER

Using a good study guide can give a student a tremendous advantage over the student who does not use one. Organized use of a study guide encourages **active learning** instead of the rather passive reading followed by a quiet "uh-hum" to one's self, signifying "I've read it and it made sense to me." That level of interaction with the chapter material is **not** adequate for the majority of college students to make a satisfactory grade. From our experience with students, this kind of passive studying leads to an intuitive level of understanding which is so tenuous that the student cannot even verbalize the major ideas that he has read. When asked later about concepts in the chapter, the student hems and haws, struggling to put together ideas that seemed clear when he read them, but which no longer hang together. He is unable to make sense out of the fragments of memories that remain from his passive reading.

In contrast to passive learning, where the student just lets something flow through his mind, **active learning** requires the student to **produce** something from the information that he has taken in. The first step in producing something is putting the ideas into your own words. Copying voluminous notes word for word from the text usually does not produce anything but writer's cramps in your hand. On numerous occasions we have had frustrated, unsuccessful students display many pages of notes they had copied word for word from the chapter--effort that earned them next to nothing.

We feel for students who have put in these ultimately unrewarded hours of passive study, and we do our best to encourage them to use more productive methods. That is really what this little spiel is all about—to encourage you to get the most out of your study time by making yourself active in working with the ideas instead of just passively absorbing the words.

One of the best-known methods for active studying is **SQ3R— Survey, Question, Read, Recite, and Review**. With this approach, you begin by surveying the material to be learned. That is, you try to find out what you have to learn before you start to learn it. Do this by looking over the chapter title, subheadings, and vocabulary in the text, and reading over the objectives in the study guide. Then, turn those headings, objectives, and major ideas into questions to guide your studying. These questions should pique your curiosity to find the answers—a curious reader is a more active reader. The next step is reading, but not just passive absorption of the material. It is active investigation of the chapter, done for the purpose of answering the questions you formed in the previous step. Next, recite or tell about the information you have just learned, to see if you can express it coherently. If you have trouble doing this, you need to go back and re-read the material until you can do it well. Finally, review the chapter to make sure you have all the points down accurately and can answer questions on them.

Although the SQ3R method is a very useful approach to studying, students sometimes have trouble applying it on their own, without help, for the first time. This is where this study guide comes into the picture. The material in the study guide is organized to take advantage of the step-by-step approach used in SQ3R.

First, **AN OVERVIEW OF THE CHAPTER** gives you a preview (or **Survey**) of the chapter information. It is intended to provide a thumbnail sketch of major topics, and serves as a springboard for further study. Read this section in connection with a quick scan of the chapter's topic headings and a more detailed examination of the summary at the end of your textbook chapter.

KEY TERMS AND CONCEPTS introduces you to the new words and ideas that are important to your understanding of the chapter. Be sure you know what these terms and ideas mean as you read them in the text. If you don't understand them, take the time to find out what they mean before you go on.

CHAPTER OBJECTIVES—CHECK YOURSELF This section tells you what you need to know if you are to be competent in discussing the chapter or in taking a test on chapter material. After reviewing this section, turn the objectives into **Questions** and then, as you **Read** your chapter, read with the goal of finding the answers to those questions. In the process, you might even experience some excitement (?, well, perhaps at least a small thrill) as you succeed in answering the questions that have been developing in your mind. If you can talk intelligently about the objectives when you finish your studying, you are well on your way to making a good grade on a chapter exam.

REVIEW EXERCISE—FILL IN THE BLANKS Here is your first opportunity to check your knowledge of chapter facts and concepts. If you remember the information you have read, you should be able to fill in (**Recite**) the words that give meaning to the statements in the exercise. After you have read about a third of the chapter, try filling out the corresponding part of the review exercise. <u>Do not write in the study guide</u>. You will want to be able to test yourself again. When you are done, check the answers at the end of the study guide chapter. See what you missed and why. Then read the next third of the chapter and try filling in the blanks for that part, along with the part of the review exercise that you did earlier. Check your answers again. This time you should have improved on the part of the review exercise that you did initially. Now complete the reading of the chapter and do the complete review exercise. Seeing improvement on that first and second part of the review exercise will give you encouragement and motivation. People feel good when they see themselves making progress, so each time make sure you keep a tally of how many you got right so you can see your improvement.

The **PRACTICE EXAM** is a final **Review** of your knowledge. If your instructor uses multiple choice questions on his/her tests, these items are likely to be very similar to the questions you will have to answer in class. Take the practice exam seriously, and approach it as you would a real test. It will give you a good idea of how much you know and how much you don't know. In other words, the practice exam is a **Reality Check**--a way of confronting the facts about your knowledge. Nobody wants to be told that he doesn't know the material, but it is better to learn that unpleasant news from a study guide than from your instructor. After checking the answers at the end of the study guide chapter, go back to the text and brush up on any weak spots.

THOUGHT QUESTIONS are included in each chapter to encourage you to put some of the issues of the chapter into your own words, to apply some of these issues to your own experience, and in some cases, to have you use your knowledge to imagine answers to questions the text doesn't ask. Thought questions dealing with provocative and controversial topics may sometimes generate provocative and controversial answers. If you do not find the suggested answers at the end of the study guide chapter satisfying, feel free to produce--and justify--your own.

Occasionally, **HELPFUL HINTS** are provided. These may relate to specific chapter material, to study habits, or just to general information that may make it easier for you to successfully navigate your way through the chapter. Use the hints where you can to make your job as a student easier.

We hope you have an enjoyable and worthwhile experience in learning about **THE CHILD**. Good luck, and more importantly, good studying!

Susan J. Bothe
Gary G. Bothe

Chapter 1

Some Basic Concepts

AN OVERVIEW OF THE CHAPTER

Chapter One tells you about some of the basic issues (concepts, ideas) in the study of child development and how information is gathered on these topics.

Development is that process which changes babies into children, children into adolescents, adolescents into young adults, and young adults into mature adults. Development goes on from the time we are conceived until we die. This book is primarily concerned with development between birth and adolescence.

Since many of the ideas in this book come from research findings, you must have a basic understanding of scientific data collection and experimentation. Chapter One presents the different methods of studying child development. It also surveys the advantages and disadvantages of the various research methods.

KEY TERMS AND CONCEPTS

development
sibling
maturation
stage
transactional view
nuclear family
peers
agemates
case study
normal curve
bell-shaped curve
normally distributed
mean

motor development
representative sample
norm
variability
significant
correlational study
correlated
positive correlation
negative correlation
longitudinal study
memory span
cross-sectional study
cohort

CHAPTER OBJECTIVES--CHECK YOURSELF

By the time you've finished reading and studying this chapter, you should be able to:

1. Define development and name the two major issues in child development.

2. Name the two major factors that affect child development.

3. State the assumptions that are inherent in stage theories. Include an explanation of the distinction between qualitative differences and quantitative differences.

4. Discuss why the human species has more adaptive flexibility than other species.

5. Define and explain the three different roles the child can take in responding to his or her environment.

6. Discuss how civilization has changed in its attitudes toward children, and list some of the factors that led to the changes.

7. Describe the contributions of G. Stanley Hall, Alfred Binet, Jean Piaget, and Sigmund Freud to the study of child development.

8. Define the following terms dealing with the collection of information for scientific study: observation, case study, correlational studies, doing experiments.

9. Describe and explain normally distributed measurements.

10. Describe a representative sample of a group.

11. Explain how "significant" in research findings is the opposite of coincidence. Explain why statisticians give a probability statement about significance.

12. List the advantages and limitations of each of the research methods discussed in this chapter.

13. Discuss the ethical concerns in doing research on human beings and state what the ultimate consideration must be.

HELPFUL HINT

Your teacher will expect you to know about the examples of research discussed in the chapter. These examples were selected to demonstrate research methods and to show how research can be done well or done poorly. In addition, your teacher might expect you to remember the findings, or conclusions, of the research examples, even though the findings are not the reason for including these research examples in Chapter One.

REVIEW EXERCISE--FILL IN THE BLANKS

1. The process through which babies move to become children, adolescents, young adults, and ultimately senior adults is called _____.

2. Research in child development is historically fairly _____.

3. _____ became the goal of the _____ family in 18th century Europe. Before that, _____ reasons had been the basis of family life. In the 18th and 19th centuries, _____ led to many men working away from the home.

4. Whether or not a particular field of study is a(n) _____ depends on the methods by which it is studied.

5. In order for observation to be useful, it must be _____.

6. Stage theorists believe in a(n) _____ pattern of change and _____ differences between stages.

7. Maturation is programmed by _____.

8. Learning gives the human species more _____ than any other species.

9. A child who acts on his environment and thereby influences how the environment will affect him in the future is playing a(n) _____ role with the environment.

10. _____ is said to have begun the study of child development.

11. _____ constructed the first IQ tests in France in the 1890's.

12. A _____ is a brother or a sister.

13. The _____, or averages, found by Mary Shirley's research on _____ development in young children have been questioned for use on American babies because her measurements were not done on a(n) _____ sample.

14. How much a group of measurements are alike or different is the _____ of those measurements.

15. Height, weight, and intelligence are distributed normally. On graphs they appear as _____ curves with the _____ of the group of measurements in the center of the distribution.

16. Children in _____ studies are repeatedly measured over the years. A(n) _____ of this kind of study is that some of the subjects may not be available to finish the study. In a _____ study, groups of children of different ages are measured and compared for differences. A problem here is that people of different age groups may sometimes have had radically different experiences. This is called the _____ effect.

17. A(n) _____ generally involves only a single child who is very unusual in some way.

18. A(n) _____ is when a prediction of one number is possible because you know the other number. The higher the number of class absences, the lower the test averages are likely to be. This is an example of a(n) _____.

19. A(n) _____ is a manipulation to try to prove causality; a(n) _____ can never be used to prove causality.

20. When experimental findings are unlikely to occur by chance, statisticians say that the findings are _____.

21. Informed consent and debriefings are _____ concerns in experimentation.

PRACTICE EXAM

1. One of the first people to do research in the field of child development was _____.
   A. McGraw   B. Shirley   C. Hall   D. Clark

2. The two major questions in child development are _____.
   A. What programs maturation and is it discontinuous?
   B. What is "normal" development and why do children differ so much from one another?
   C. When will nature and nurture merge and will that merger produce a cohort effect?
   D. Does development influence the transactional process and should the nuclear family be included?

3. Which of the following is NOT an assumption of stage theory?
   A. Changes between stages are qualitative.
   B. Quantitative maturation is flexible.
   C. Transitions from stage to stage may not be sharp and clear cut.
   D. Stages have a certain order in which they will happen.

4

4. Human flexibility _____.
   A. has four stages of qualitative change
   B. defines the nature-nurture issue
   C. reinforces the contrast effect
   D. permits adaptation to a wide range of possible
      environments

5. When child and environment affect each other, this is
   called a _____ view of development.
   A. reactional   C. maturational
   B. transactional   D. cohort

6. Whether or not something is a science depends on _____.
   A. what is being studied
   B. how something is being studied
   C. who is conducting the study
   D. whether it is done in a FDA licensed laboratory

7. Which of the following is an example of discontinuous
   change?
   A. the temperature in your home
   B. your checking account balance
   C. your body weight
   D. the amount of water in your bathtub

8. In Mary Shirley's study of motor development of infants,
   _____.
   A. results were based on babies from too many cultures
   B. the results could be applied to all babies
   C. the norms still agree with updated norms
   D. the norms are applicable to white babies of Northern
      European ancestry

9. A representative sample contains _____.
   A. one uniform type of individual
   B. children of one sex at a time
   C. persons with the same characteristics, and in the same
      percentages, as is found in the rest of the population
   D. only those individuals defined as "average"

10. In a normal distribution _____.
    A. the mean is on the right-hand side
    B. measurements at the mean or close to it are common
    C. "normal" is precisely defined
    D. only information from FDA research is acceptable

11. The normal distribution curve is _____ in appearance.
    A. a circle   C. flipped up on the ends
    B. bell-shaped   D. a hyperbolic triangle

12. The "average child" _____.
    A. does not exist, except in theoretical terms
    B. is usually average in everything
    C. matures more quickly than most children
    D. must be used in child development experiments

13. Norms are useful to parents because _____.
   A. they give a general idea of the ages for certain behaviors to appear
   B. they indicate the precise age when a behavior will appear
   C. they define "abnormal" as any behavior that appears two weeks after the mean age for onset
   D. they allow parents to properly program their child's behavior

14. The discontinuous pattern of infant intellectual development evidenced by the results of intelligence tests may be the result of _____.
   A. slow maturation
   B. the transactional process
   C. lack of adequate research technology to study infant intelligence
   D. use of biased representative samples

15. In a cross-sectional developmental study, _____.
   A. individuals of different ages are compared
   B. each subject is studied for an extended period of years
   C. one of the big problems is the drop-out rate
   D. more than one experimenter is required

16. Child development research need not involve measurements and comparisons between children of different ages. Sometimes it just involves _____.
   A. the experimental method   C. correlational studies
   B. observation and description D. ethical considerations

17. A positive correlation would likely be found between _____.
   A. number miles driven and amount of gas left in the tank
   B. temperature outside and amount of clothing worn
   C. number of long distance calls and amount of phone bill
   D. human height and hair color

18. To determine the direction of causality _____.
   A. do a correlation
   B. do an experiment
   C. do a case study
   D. revise the assumptions about the direction of causality

19. Statisticians will generally label any result that has less than a .05 probability of being coincidence as being _____.
   A. significant   C. insignificant
   B. not significant   D. random

20. Deception is _____.
    A. never justified as an experimental tool
    B. justifiable to keep a subject participating in
       an experiment
    C. justifiable only when it is the only way worthwhile
       research can be done
    D. the most common way developmental research is done

21. Imagine that children who were at a very "impressionable
    age" at the time of the Challenger disaster have increased
    apprehension about manned space exploration. This would
    show up in cross-sectional research about attitudes on the
    space program as a _____ effect.
    A. longitudinal
    B. variability
    C. correlated
    D. cohort

22. You discover that you will have access to 200 children for
    the next five years. You realize you cannot let this
    opportunity go to waste, so you start planning a _____
    study.
    A. variability   C. cross-sectional
    B. longitudinal   D. cohort

23. The efforts of _____ led to the construction of the first
    IQ tests in the _____.
    A. Freud, 1930's   C. Piaget, 1900's
    B. Binet, 1890's   D. Hall, 1920's

24. A new measure for intelligence for babies is the baby's
    _____.
    A. head size   C. visual acuity
    B. onset of boredom   D. activity index

25. An indication of variability is the _____.
    A. size of the representative sample
    B. difference between the smallest and largest
       measurements
    C. number of norms present
    D. size of the mean

26. Ethical considerations are ultimately made on the basis of
    _____.
    A. the subject's informed consent
    B. potential benefits of the research weighed against
       possible harm or deception for the subject
    C. the cost of rehabilitation for the subject if harm
       comes to her, and if funds will be available for that
       rehabilitation
    D. whether the researcher feels morally comfortable with
       the procedures of the experiment

27. In Muir and Field's sound localization research, they made sure the observers recording the baby's behaviors could not hear the sound to prevent _____.
    A. the observers from being biased by their own expectations
    B. the observers from unintentionally giving the babies clues
    C. the researchers from subtly influencing the observers
    D. the babies from influencing the observer's behaviors

28. A correlational study would be the research method of choice when _____.
    A. a representative sample is not available
    B. there are only a limited number of subjects available
    C. the variable that you want to study is not under your control
    D. the subjects are available for a limited time only

29. One of the disadvantages of a cross-sectional study is

    _____.
    A. cohort effect   C. lack of maturation
    B. loss of subjects   D. practice effects

30. With the current greater awareness of the transactional nature of the parent-child relationship, _____.
    A. there is a new emphasis on research to alter the genetic temperament of the baby
    B. fathers are being encouraged to be in the delivery room
    C. parents are being asked to make earlier decisions about the child's future
    D. parents are no longer seen as the total determinants of the parent-child interaction

THOUGHT QUESTIONS

1. Imagine that you want to study the growth of vocabulary in children between the ages of two and four years. Would you choose a cross-sectional study or a longitudinal study? Give the advantages and disadvantages of each design.

2. Using examples from everyday life, explain why it is said that a correlation between two variables does not prove a cause and effect relationship between the two variables.

3. If your friend calls you with concern over the fact that her 15-month-old baby is not yet walking, what would you say to her? Use the terms "norm" and "variability".

4. Do you believe the potential benefits of research in child development warrant the use of deception by the researcher? How can you support your answer?

ANSWERS WITH PAGE REFERENCES

Fill in the Blanks

1. development (2)
2. new (10)
3. mutual affection (10)
   nuclear (10)
   economic (10)
   industrialization (10)
4. science (9)
5. systematic (9)
6. discontinuous (7)
   qualitative (7)
7. genes (8)
8. adaptive flexibility (8)
9. transactional (9)
10. G. Stanley Hall (10)
11. Alfred Binet (11)
12. sibling (3)
13. norms (16)

   motor (16)
   representative (15-16)
14. variability (16)
15. bell-shaped (13)
   mean (13)
16. longitudinal (23)
   disadvantage (23)
   cross-sectional (23)
   cohort (24)
17. case study (13)
18. correlation (21)
   negative correlation (21)
19. experiment (16-18, 21)
   correlations (23)
20. significant (21)
21. ethical (19)

Multiple Choice

1. C (10)	9. C (16)	17. C (21)	25. B (16)
2. B (2)	10. B (13-14)	18. B (21-25)	26. B (19)
3. B (7-8)	11. B (13)	19. A (21)	27. A (20)
4. D (8)	12 A (14)	20. C (19)	28. C (21)
5. B (9)	13. A (16)	21. D (29)	29. A (24)
6. B (9)	14. C (6-7)	22. B (23)	30. D (25)
7. B (7)	15. A (23)	23. B (11)	
8. D (16)	16. B (11)	24. B (7)	

SUGGESTED ANSWERS TO THOUGHT QUESTIONS

1. The main advantage of a cross-sectional study is that it can be done in a short period of time. The major disadvantage is that cohort effects may be present which may distort the data. The main advantage of a longitudinal study is that subjects can serve as their own controls. The major disadvantages are that subjects may no longer be available as the study proceeds over time, the results may be biased because of some selection factor which might influence which subjects continue to be available and, longitudinal studies take much longer than cross-sectional studies.

2. There is likely a strong positive correlation between number of gallons of gasoline bought and number of hamburgers bought. It hardly makes sense to say that gasoline causes hamburgers, or vice versa, so the existence of the correlation says nothing about cause and effect. It

is likely, though, that there is a third factor responsible for both of the first two factors: traveling away from home.

3. I would tell her norms are averages made over a wide range of scores. For instance, if you have a 10-month-old beginning walker and a 14-month-old beginning walker, the average is 12 months which is 2 months away from either. Thus there is a certain amount of variability among the scores used to determine a norm. Not being precisely on the norm does not make one "abnormal."

4. You might make one or more of the following arguments: No—people should NEVER be deceived, no matter how good the reason. It is a matter of moral behavior.
No—people who are deceived may never trust another experimenter, and if they find out they were deceived during the study, their data may be distorted.
Yes—if there is informed consent and the person is fully debriefed after the experiment.
Yes—in a long term longitudinal study when full knowledge would affect the subject's behavior.
Yes—if there is informed consent, even though the debriefing is on a limited basis and the long term deception is protective to the subject.

Chapter 2

Heredity and Environment

AN OVERVIEW OF THE CHAPTER

Chapter Two tells how heredity and environment affect the development of the child. Most experts agree that children are affected by both; however, how much each contributes and how they interact is hotly debated. The long-standing debate over which is more important is known as the "nature-nurture" issue. The chapter discusses the environmental influences first. Then it discusses how heredity works, and finally it considers how genes and environment interact, each impacting on the other.

Environment refers to everything a person is exposed to after his genetic pattern is determined at the time of conception. It includes everything that a person sees, hears, feels, smells, and tastes. It also includes the culture(s) of the society(s) to which the child is exposed. Of particular interest to child development researchers are the diverse child rearing practices seen in different societies. Your textbook explores some of the elements of American society that affect today's child: different socioeconomic levels, major changes in the American family structure, and the frequency of child abuse.

The next section explains how genes and chromosomes relate to heredity and different types of genetic and chromosomal abnormalities. The possibilities that genetic counseling offer are also discussed.

Finally, in the section on the interaction of heredity and environment, the authors report on the types of research used in the attempt to determine which are the effects of heredity and which are the effects of environment. They also point out three ways in which what appear to be environmental effects may actually be determined by genetics.

KEY TERMS AND CONCEPTS

heredity
environment
nature
nurture
culture
society
subculture
socioeconomic status
genes
DNA
chromosomes
sex chromosomes
PKU
recessive trait
dominant trait
carrier
mutation
sex-linked trait
Down syndrome
amniocentesis
trisomy 21
chorionic villus sampling
fragile X syndrome

polygenic trait
passive effects
reactive effects
active effects
controlled
inbred
identical twins
monozygotic twins
fraternal twins
dizygotic twins
heritability
biological parents
temperament
contrast effect
hyperactivity
conduct disorder
depression
anxiety disorder
obsessive-compulsive disorder
autism
childhood schizophrenia
transactional view

CHAPTER OBJECTIVES--CHECK YOURSELF

By the time you've finished reading and studying this chapter, you should be able to:

1. Describe the nature-nurture debate.

2. List some developmental factors that are environmental influences.

3. Contrast the goals of communal societies (China and the Israeli kibbutz) with those of American society.

4. Explain how socioeconomic status may affect a child more than his/her cultural background.

5. List ways in which the traditional American family has changed.

6. Summarize the possible effects that living in a single parent home can have on the child.

7. Describe the problem of child abuse.

8. Summarize the impact of siblings on the child. Include research findings on birth order, family size, and relationships with siblings.

9. Explain how the heredity of a baby (including sex) is determined at conception.

10. Explain the workings of dominant and recessive genes.

11. Explain the workings of sex-linked disorders.

12. Describe the characteristics and causes of Down syndrome.

13. Explain how single-gene traits are different from polygenic traits and give some examples of each.

14. Explain how heredity and environment interact to produce characteristics.

15. Explain how the vicious circle of reactive effects may work to "normalize" a child's behavior, or may work to make a bad situation worse.

16. Describe the research findings on intelligence and the nature-nurture debate.

17. Discuss the use of identical twins and adopted children in research on heredity and environment.

18. Describe evidence supporting the idea that temperament is genetically determined.

19. Explain how the contrast effect can make identical twins become different from each other.

20. Explain where the psychiatric disorders discussed in Box 2-4 fit into the nature-nurture debate.

HELPFUL HINTS

1. Your instructor may want you to know all the specific contents of tables; ask what amount of detail you are to know from the tables. You certainly are expected to be able to state the overall concept that the table is displaying.

2. Review all terms and concepts from the previous chapter(s) even if they are not to be formally covered on the test.

3. I call to your attention again that in the nature-nurture debate NATURE IS NOT ENVIRONMENT. Students readily confuse these perhaps because the current need to save the environment means trying to protect the elements of Nature.

REVIEW EXERCISE--FILL IN THE BLANKS

1. Children are shaped by two forces: their _____ and their _____. Psychologists have debated for years over which of these two most determine which characteristics the person will have. This is called the _____ debate. _____ refers to the way a child is raised and what he/she experiences.

2. A _____ is a group of people with a common culture.

3. A family's _____ depends on the income, profession, education and social status of its members. New research suggests that a young child's wellbeing seems to be more determined by the _____ of his family rather than his _____.

4. The family of an abused child is likely to be a family under _____. Families in _____ are more likely to experience this.

5. As adults, the victims of child abuse are more likely than others to suffer from _____, _____ and _____.

6. Inherited characteristics are transmitted by, _____ which are made of _____. These form long chains in very specific orders called _____.

7. A genetically normal human has _____ chromosomes. A child receives _____ chromosomes from his mother and _____ chromosomes from his father.

8. When the two genes in a pair do not match, the _____ gene wins. It shows up in _____ who inherits that gene. Genes which have to match up to show are called _____ genes.

9. The traits that women rarely show but may carry and pass to their sons are called _____. They are carried on the _____ chromosomes. One such disorder is _____.

10. A fatal inherited metabolic disorder carried by recessive genes which destroys the brain by a buildup of fat molecules is _____.

11. A trait that depends on more than one pair of genes is called _____.

12. Interactions between heredity and environment are extremely _____.

13. _____ twins are formed when one fertilized egg splits to form two separate people. Each one of these people possess _____ chromosomes. Another name for this type of twin is _____. _____ twins (also called _____), result when two separate eggs are fertilized by two separate sperm.

14. The _____ is the increase in small differences between twins because families have noticed these differences and emphasized them.

15. _____ children are those that a person gets through marriage to one of the legal parents of those children.

16. The view that there is a two-way interaction between the child and the environment is called a _____ approach to the study of child development.

PRACTICE EXAM

1. The nature-nurture controversy is a debate over _____.
   A. whether mothers should work outside the home
   B. the difference between nature and genetics
   C. which is more important--heredity or environment
   D. the best way to determine a child's nutritional needs

2. A person's language, beliefs, and values are his _____.
   A. culture   C. personality
   B. society   D. heredity

3. The death rate for children in the U.S. resulting from physical abuse or neglect is _____.
   A. one per week
   B. three per day
   C. ten per day
   D. one every ninety minutes

4. Cultural differences may be diminishing in the world because of _____.
   A. the growing advances in child development research
   B. technological advances and increasing contact with other societies
   C. maturation reaching its biological limit
   D. increasing emphasis on existential psychology

5. When observing an event, you must know the _____ to understand the event.
   A. cohort   C. chorion
   B. correlation   D. context

6. The Eskimo child was not upset about being asked to die so the aunt could have the shirt because _____.
   A. the child perceived it as fun teasing
   B. death over clothes is a reality of Eskimo culture
   C. Eskimo children have a rare recessive gene that reduces emotionality
   D. the chorionic effect is most clearly seen in Eskimo society

7. A trait that depends on more than one pair of genes
   is called _____.
   A. dominant   C. polygenic
   B. recessive   D. multimutant

8. If you want to reduce child abuse, which of the following
   acts would probably be the most beneficial?
   A. Eliminate poverty.
   B. Pass tougher laws against child abuse.
   C. Pass laws against remarriage to eliminate stepparents.
   D. Teach parents what children are really like.

9. In sexual reproduction, the father _____.
   A. passes sex-linked traits to his sons
   B. causes the multimutations
   C. carries the dominant genes
   D. determines the sex of the offspring

10. The correlation in IQ scores for identical twins is _____.
    A. high
    B. the same as for balanced socioeconomic groups
    C. the same as for fraternal twins
    D. the same as for randomly matched individuals

11. When first-born children are compared to their siblings,
    the first-born tend to be _____.
    A. low achievers   C. more verbal
    B. more social   D. more self-confident

12. The new view of the interaction between heredity and
    environment is that _____.
    A. heredity is most important
    B. environment is most important
    C. heredity and environment interact in a complex way
    D. it is a multimutant process

13. Children have the genetic material of their _____.
    A. adoptive parents   C. foster parents
    B. biological parents D. stepparents

14. "Difficult" children _____.
    A. have been exposed to chorionic villus sampling
    B. tend to sleep long hours
    C. are slow to adapt to change
    D. have the PKU recessive trait

15. One fact which makes it difficult to separate the effects
    of heredity and environment on intelligence is that _____.
    A. identical twins have identical heredity
    B. fraternal twins experience identical environment
    C. siblings who have the same environments turn out the
       same
    D. people who have the same inheritance often share
       similar environments.

16. The differences between the children of employed mothers and those of mothers who stay at home have been shown to _____.
    A. be of little importance   C. be highly significant
    B. lead to norm deviations   D. lead to sex-linked traits

17. A child with _____ is mentally retarded, has a short neck, small head, stubby fingers, thin hair, and a large tongue.
    A. Down syndrome   C. amniocentesis
    B. Tay-Sachs disease   D. fragile X disorder

18. Parental divorce _____.
    A. has little impact on the child unless that child was already emotionally disturbed
    B. always brings a more tranquil environment because the parents stop fighting
    C. brings a considerable amount of grief, anger, and anxiety to the child who may or may not eventually resolve these feelings
    D. helps the child by raising the socioeconomic level of both of the two resulting households

19. The stepchild-stepparent relationship that has the best chance of working is one where _____.
    A. there are stepchildren from both sides of the marriage living in the home on a continuing basis
    B. the stepchild is old enough so (s)he can understand the new family relationships
    C. the child is a girl who will tend to romanticize the relationship between her parent and stepparent
    D. the child is quite young

20. When fathers get custody of their children, _____.
    A. sex-linked disorders are likely to develop
    B. sex-linked disorders are less likely to develop
    C. the divorce is likely to be friendlier and therefore less traumatic to the children
    D. the child is less likely to suffer the effects of poverty

21. As a person gets older, there may be increasing genetic impact as compared to environmental impact because _____.
    A. the genes mature
    B. the person has more freedom to actively select his environment
    C. he is likely to become sexually active which will increase his chromosome count
    D. his chromosomes start to double to prevent sex-linked disorders in his children

22. An example of a transactional pattern between the child and his environment is seen in the _____ effect.
    A. polygenic   C. contrast
    B. Down's   D. autism

17

23. A latchkey child is one who _____.
    A. is adopted
    B. has two stepparents
    C. was a foster child before he was adopted
    D. stays without adult supervision after school until
       parents come home from work

24. Most of the psychiatric disorders of children discussed in
    Chapter Two seem to be the result of _____.
    A. a dominant gene
    B. a recessive gene
    C. the environment
    D. a combination of genetic and environmental factors

25. Children who are born with very sensitive nervous systems
    and who tend to have hair-trigger reactions to stress are
    likely to be _____ children.
    A. resilient   C. shy, inhibited
    B. normalized   D. contrast

26. According to your text, which of the following actions
    would most benefit the world's children?
    A. Raise the socioeconomic status of families.
    B. Adopt the indulgent-mother parenting style of the
       traditional Chinese family.
    C. Reduce world cultural differences.
    D. Make sure all children live in technologically advanced
       societies.

27. The birth arrangement that seems to be the most
    advantageous to a child's overall intellectual development
    is for the child to be _____.
    A. oldest in a very large family
    B. youngest in a family of three children
    C. the older of two children born four years apart
    D. an only child

28. Who is most likely to be responsible for abuse of children?
    Who is the second most frequent child abuser statistically?
    A. foster parents; birth parents
    B. parents; a man other than the father
    C. siblings 5 years or older than the victim; fathers
    D. fathers; neighbors

29. The most common factor usually seen in the homes where
    abuse happens is _____.
    A. parents who are overeducated
    B. alcoholism
    C. mental illness
    D. poverty

30. Which of the following would be an example of an "active" genetic effect, according to Scarr and McCarthy?
    A. The child drags home broken mechanical objects to repair.
    B. A father brings home mechanical toys for his son because he believes boys are born mechanically minded.
    C. A child sees his father fixing mechanical objects.
    D. The boy's sister asks him to fix her bicycle.

THOUGHT QUESTIONS

1. List four characteristics about yourself and discuss how you might have acquired each of these. Use the terms heredity and environment in your discussion.

2. List values that you want to teach your children. Are these part of your culture?

3. Consider your family or another one that you know well. How has it been impacted by American cultural changes?

4. When planning your family, how will the information in this chapter influence the number and spacing of your children?

5. Some states have laws that determine how closely related relatives can be and still marry. Does this chapter suggest some reasons why such laws might have been made? Support your answer with facts from the chapter.

ANSWERS WITH PAGE REFERENCES

Fill in the Blanks

1. heredity (30)
   environment (30)
   nature-nurture (30)
   nurture (30)
2. society (31)
3. socioeconomic level (35)
   socioeconomic level (35)
   culture (35)
4. stress (38)
   poverty (38)
5. depression (39)
   low self esteem (39)
   difficulty in trusting others (39)
6. genes (48)
   DNA (48)
   chromosomes (48)
7. 46 (48)
   23 (48)
   23 (48)
8. dominant (49)
   everyone (49)
   recessive (49)
9. sex-linked (50)
   sex (50)
   color-blindness (50), or
   hemophilia (51), or
   Duchenne muscular dystrophy (51)
10. Tay-Sachs (54)
11. polygenic (55-56)
12. complex (74)

13. Identical (60)   14. contrast effect (71)
    46 (60)   15. stepchildren (44)
    monozygotic (60)   16. transactional (74)
    fraternal (60)
    dizygotic (60)

Multiple Choice

1.	C (30)	9.	D (49)	17.	A (51)	25.	C (67)
2.	A (31)	10.	A (61)	18.	C (42)	26.	A (35)
3.	B (38)	11.	C (46)	19.	D (44)	27.	C (46)
4.	B (35)	12.	C (74)	20.	D (43)	28.	B (38)
5.	D (31)	13.	B (63)	21.	B (62)	29.	D (38)
6.	A (31)	14.	C (68)	22.	C (71)	30.	A (59)
7.	C (55)	15.	D (61)	23.	D (41)		
8.	A (38)	16.	A (37)	24.	D (73)		

SUGGESTED ANSWERS TO THOUGHT QUESTIONS

1. The following characteristics are among those you may have chosen:
    eye color - genetic, but perhaps altered with contact lens
    hair color - genetic, but perhaps deliberately altered
        with chemicals or incidentally altered by sun and
        chlorine of swimming pools
    activity level - Temperament is genetically determined, but
        environmental factors can influence that temperament.
        Chemicals that are inhaled or ingested (alcohol, lead
        from auto emissions, sugar, caffeine) alter brain
        activity. Environmental consequences (rewards or
        punishments) may lead one to suppress or accentuate
        aspects of temperament.
    intelligence - Potential seems to be genetically set, but
        environment will determine how much of that potential
        will be manifested. A brief episode   of oxygen
        deprivation can forever alter brain capabilities.
        Malnutrition and an impoverished environment impair
        intellectual function. Exposure to pollutants such as
        lead can retard development. An enriched environment
        with optimal stimulation and reinforcement of
        intellectual pursuits would tend to maximize
        intellectual potential.

2. Here is a list of possible values. Consider which two or
    three are most important to you: independence, self
    reliance, sociability, gregariousness, education emphasis,
    materialism, spiritualism, athletics, art and/or music
    appreciation, neatness, church attendance, individualism,
    environmental concerns, cleanliness, stylishness, and
    integrity.

3. Issues you might consider are:
    divorce - children living in single-parent homes or in
        blended families with a stepparent
    women in the work force - children in day care or latchkey
        arrangements
    single mothers - children in single-parent homes of mothers
        who have chosen not to marry

4. The optimal intellectual environment is to have one or two
    children spaced 3 or 4 years apart. Then invite a younger
    child over for the only or second child to be "teacher" to.
    For sibling relationships, same-sexed siblings seem to get
    along better than opposite-sexed siblings, particularly as
    they get older.

5. Most undesirable genes are recessive, which means both
    parents must carry a specific gene for it to show in the
    offspring. The closer the kinship is, the more the
    persons share the same gene pool which increases the
    likelihood that both parents will have the undesirable gene
    to pass to an offspring.

Chapter 3

Theories of Development

AN OVERVIEW OF THE CHAPTER

Chapter Three describes the most well known theories of human development. The chapter begins with a history of the ideas that have led to modern developmental psychology. John Locke's idea that the environment determines the child and Jean-Jacques Rousseau's idea that the child is better off uncorrupted by its environment tell us that the nature-nurture debate has been around a long time. Charles Darwin's idea that human behavior can be studied by scientific methods (discussed in Chapter One), encouraged the pursuit of knowledge about child development through systematic observation and experimentation. The other popular method of pursuing knowledge in the early years was a philosophical approach, which involved logical thinking about a topic instead of making observations and doing experiments.

The rest of the chapter consists of brief descriptions of major theories in child development. After explaining that theories are used to make sense out of a collection of information, the authors present the psychoanalytic theories of Sigmund Freud and Erik Erikson, which focus on emotions and relationships.

Discussed next are four theories based on learning: classical behaviorism, neobehaviorism, social learning theory, and social cognitive theory. Classical behaviorism was founded by men who were looking for natural laws that determine how a person behaves. These early behaviorists were not interested in emotions, relationships or thoughts. Their basic attitude was that if something can't be seen, counted or measured, scientists (psychologists) shouldn't try to work with it.

Psychologists who agree with the principles of learning but do not adhere to the hardnosed approach demanding only observable events are called neobehaviorists. In their study of learning, they not only look at observable behaviors, but are also willing to consider events that are not observable, such as thoughts and feelings.

Social learning theory says one can learn without having to actually experience external reinforcement and punishment. One need only watch someone else have the experience. It is called social learning theory because it takes place in a social context; by definition, at least two people are required for it to occur.

A newer version of social learning theory moves the focus to thinking, reasoning, and the understanding of our own experience with rewards and punishments. Although the basics of learning theory are still accepted, the major emphasis is on self-reflective thinking (cognition) instead of on watching someone else. With the emphasis on cognition, the new theory is called social-cognitive theory.

The next theories discussed are purely cognitive, not partially based on learning theory as social cognitive theory is. Cognitive processes include such things as thinking, planning, and building new ideas. Feelings and emotions are not considered. Jean Piaget is a giant among cognitive developmental theorists.

Information processing is the other purely cognitive theory discussed. Information processing portrays the working of the human mind in terms similar to those used by computer scientists. Robbie Case has developed a new theory that brings together the ideas of Piaget, information-processing and emotional development.

Kohlberg's stage theory of moral development is outlined in a special-interest box.

The last two theories in the chapter are biological theories--ethology and sociobiology. They address inborn behaviors and behaviors that lead to survival. These are not presently central viewpoints in child development.

The chapter ends by emphasizing the question that naive psychology students often ask. "Which theory is right?" Ultimate truth is very complex; so far we cannot prove that any of the theories in this chapter has the "right" answer. Searching for ultimate truth is done by eliminating ideas that can be proven wrong. We are then left to continue testing and refining the remaining ideas. Some very early theories have been proven wrong. The remaining theories each have strengths and weaknesses. Theories are not necessarily incompatible with one another. Some focus on entirely different aspects of development. Sometimes theories are brought together and combined to more effectively predict and explain behaviors.

KEY TERMS AND CONCEPTS

cognitive development
preformation
doctrine of innate ideas
tabula rasa
instinct
species-specific behavior
psychoanalytic theory
psychoanalysis
hysterical symptom
traumatic
id
drive
ego
superego
repressed
displaced
displaced aggression
reaction formation
oral stage
anal stage
fixated
phallic stage
castration
Oedipal conflict
Electra conflict
penis envy
identify
latency period
genital stage
psychosocial
psychosexual
basic trust
autonomy
ego growth
identity crisis
ego integrity
behaviorism
stimulus
response
visual stimulus
auditory stimulus

organism
condition
pairing
conditioned fear
phobia
preparedness
prepared
Skinner box
classical conditioning
operant conditioning
reflex
reinforcer
reinforce
reinforcement
extinction
extinguish
partial reinforcement
shaping
punishment
model
modeling
vicarious reinforcement
vicarious punishment
cognition
adaptation
scheme
object permanence
representations
deferred imitation
egocentric
conservation
center
decenter
preconventional moral
   reasoning
conventional moral reasoning
postconventional moral
   reasoning
information processing
encoding
automatization
ethology

CHAPTER OBJECTIVES--CHECK YOURSELF

By the time you've finished reading and studying this chapter, you should be able to:

1. Explain the purpose of theories in scientific pursuits.

2. Summarize the early ideas about childhood. Include preformation and the doctrine of innate ideas, Locke and Rousseau.

3. Discuss Freud's theory of personality development.

4. List Erikson's eight stages of development and the basic theme (conflict) of each stage.

5. Compare and contrast Freud and Erikson.

6. Give a brief overview of behaviorism, naming its major contributors.

7. List and describe the four lines of theory that are based on learning principles.

8. Describe Ivan Pavlov's experiment and connect it historically to behaviorism.

9. Describe Watson's famous experiment and explain why it is unethical by today's standards.

10. Explain the process of operant conditioning; include the terms reinforcer, punishment, extinction, and shaping.

11. Compare and contrast social learning theory and social cognitive theory.

12. Describe the three theories given in this chapter to explain phobias.

13. Discuss Piaget's theory of cognitive development and list his four stages.

14. Discuss Kohlberg's stages of moral development and the research relevant to them.

15. Summarize the main ideas of information-processing theory.

16. Compare and contrast Piaget's and Case's theories.

17. Describe the two biological theories found in Chapter 3.

HELPFUL HINTS

1. Learn all the names of the major theorists discussed in Chapter Three; LEARN them. They will appear over and over, so learn them NOW if you do not know them from earlier psych courses. They are part of the ABC's of psychology.

2. Etch into your brain that behaviorism means learning.
   Every time you hear the word behaviorism "learning" should
   pop into your mind.

3. Ask if you need to know the text material about the
   personal lives of the major theorists for test purposes.
   For some of you, the personal histories will make
   remembering the theorists and their theories easier. The
   personal lives of some of these theorists reveal them to be
   very colorful, memorable people. There are several
   recounted in this chapter whose lives would make excellent
   soap operas for television.

4. Review the material in Chapter One on stage theories since
   the psychoanalytic theorists (Freud and Erikson), and the
   cognitive theorist (Piaget), Case's theory of cognitive and
   emotional development, and the theorist in moral
   development (Kohlberg) are all stage theorists.

REVIEW EXERCISE--FILL IN THE BLANKS

1. A prevailing idea in the ancient world was _____, the
   assumption that an extremely small "grownup" was contained
   in the egg or sperm, and that this tiny creature just grew
   into the adult it was destined to become.

2. John Locke believed that the mind of a newborn baby is a
   _____, an "empty slate," which is a _____ viewpoint in the
   nature—nurture debate.

3. Rousseau believed that children are born good and should be
   left alone to develop naturally. Rousseau claimed that
   civilized _____ is responsible for corrupting people.

4. _____ made human behavior a proper subject for a natural
   science.

5. Darwin believed that "instincts," now called _____
   behaviors, are inherited in the same way as physical
   features.

6. Freud named his method for analyzing the mind _____.

7. According to Freud, the human mind consists of three
   different "agencies" or aspects. They are the _____,
   _____, and _____. The _____, present from birth is the
   home of powerful instinctive desires. Through experience
   with reality the young baby starts to develop the _____,
   the thinking mind. The _____ is in favor of what society
   regards as "good" behavior.

8. Forbidden thoughts are _____ or _____.

9. In Freudian theory there are _____ stages. The first one, the _____ stage, focuses on the mouth. During the second stage, or _____, the major focus is learning to control the bowels, or potty-training.

10. During the _____ stage, attention is focused on the pleasurable sensations produced in the genitals. Electra and Oedipal conflicts are resolved when the child begins to _____ with the parent of the same sex.

11. During the latency _____ (not _____), all sexual feelings are repressed; girls play mainly with girls and boys with boys.

12. In the _____ stage, which should begin with adolescence, adult-like love relationships with persons of the opposite sex develop.

13. Erikson's theory is similar to Freud's; but Erikson places more emphasis on _____ and has _____ stages while Freud has only _____ stages and one _____. Also, Freud sees development as finished by adolescence; Erikson sees it as continuing _____.

14. _____ are interested in what events control behavior. They are not interested in what their subjects think or feel; they will discuss only observable events. _____, also called _____, adhere to the principles of learning, but they will consider events that cannot be seen.

15. Of the two basic types of learning, _____ is based on training a reflex to appear in response to a new stimulus, such as a cat salivating when she hears the can opener because in her experience, food comes after the can opener sound. The second type of learning is called _____. It is the change in behavior that comes because of the consequences (payoffs) that result when the organism does the behavior.

16. Anything that will increase the likelihood that a behavior will occur again is called a _____. A negative stimulus used to decrease the likelihood that a behavior will occur again is called a _____.

17. If reinforcement has been given in an off-and-on manner, it is said to be _____ reinforcement. If an animal has experienced this and is then put into the process of _____, where it gets no reinforcement at all, it will continue to do the behavior much longer than if it has experienced _____ reinforcement.

18. According to learning theory, there are three methods for curing a phobia. Two of these are _____ and _____.

19. Social _____ theorists believe that much of human behavior is acquired by observing another person's behavior.

20. _____ development is the development of the ability to think, to reason, and to understand.

21. In social _____ theory there is increased emphasis on thinking. In this theory, Bandura says the person learns by observing the results of _____ behavior.

22. Social cognitive theory is actually more like _____ than like cognitive theory in _____ ways. Cognitive theories focus entirely on what the child thinks, whereas social cognitive theory the focus is on what the child actually _____ and the _____ of that behavior. Also, social learning theory is like behaviorism in that development is a _____ process, while cognitive theory sees development as happening in _____.

23. Piaget's _____ period begins at birth and lasts until age 18 - 24 months. The most important cognitive development of this stage is _____. In the preoperational stage, the child develops increasing ability to use _____ thought although he is still _____, unable to see a situation from anyone's point of view but his own.

24. In Piaget's period of _____ operations, a child can consider only events that he can experience through his five senses. Only when the period of _____ operations is reached can a person do _____ thinking where nontouchable ideas can be considered.

25. _____ extended Piaget's theory and developed a theory of _____ levels of moral development. Further research suggests there may be an important _____ difference that was not initially considered in these levels of moral development. Your authors make an important point that this difference is statistically _____, but not indicated in every case for specific individuals.

26. Information-processing theory considers how information is _____ taken in and what processes happen to it once it is in. The information can be _____, _____ in memory, _____ from memory, and _____ again.

27. Information-processing considers the mind to work as a _____ has been built to work. The "hardware" of the system is the _____ features of the brain. The "software" is the learned _____ for using the mind's capacity.

28. In Robbie Case's theory, _____ theory and _____ theory have been brought together. Emotional development is also included. Case's theory sees development in _____, as Piaget's theory does. This is unlike most _____ theories.

29. Biological theories focus primarily on _____ behaviors. The two biological theories described in this chapter are _____ and _____. _____ is the study of species-specific behaviors (also known as _____). _____ believe the ultimate purpose of all activities is the survival of genes, and that the _____ are directing these activities.

PRACTICE EXAM

1. A "good" theory serves to _____.
   A. organize and summarize observations
   B. reinforce what we already believe
   C. automatize schema production
   D. reduce focus on specific topics

2. A "wrong" theory is _____.
   A. destructive to scientific pursuits
   B. leads to preformation
   C. useful if it allows researchers to prove something untrue, thus moving closer to what is true
   D. one that is illegal because it was produced outside of a FDA licensed laboratory

3. Jean-Jacques Rousseau would be most in favor of _____.
   A. mandatory kindergarten attendance
   B. required school attendance until age 16
   C. parentally supervised home schooling
   D. letting children determine their own education

4. The person who talked about inherited behaviors was _____.
   A. Locke   C. Gestalt
   B. Skinner   D. Darwin

5. According to Freud, which aspect of the mind wants immediate gratification?
   A. superego   B. sexual   C. id   D. ego

6. Freud's first stage of development was _____.
   A. anal   B. oral   C. genital   D. phallic

7. During the _____ stage, children experience their Oedipal and Electra conflicts.
   A. genital   B. latency   C. phallic   D. oral

8. Freud would say which aspect of the mind houses the conscience?
   A. phallus   B. superego   C. operant   D. ego

9. Erik Erikson places more emphasis than Freud on _____.
   A. stages   C. genetics
   B. sexuality   D. social interactions

29

10. Autonomy, in Erikson's second stage, refers to _____.
    A. basic trust in the caretaker
    B. independence and individuality
    C. developing identity
    D. generating integrity

11. According to stage theorists, _____.
    A. each stage is a bigger and better version of the
       previous stage
    B. each stage is qualitatively different from the
       previous stage
    C. the rate at which children achieve stages is universal
    D. the sequence of stages varies from child to child

12. According to Piaget, schemes are _____.
    A. patterns of action   C. species-specific
    B. part of tabula rasa   D. based on the id

13. During Piaget's sensorimotor period, the child's major
    accomplishment is development of _____.
    A. logical reasoning   C. egocentrism
    B. a sense of an identity   D. object permanence

14. According to Kohlberg's moral theory, _____.
    A. most U.S. citizens remain in level one
    B. all normal adults progress to level three
    C. the majority of U.S. citizens live in level two
    D. moral level is based on IQ

15. Skinner's and Watson's theories are _____ theories.
    A. Freudian   C. cognitive
    B. behavioristic   D. stage

16. Pavlov's classical conditioning was based on _____.
    A. extinction of neutral behaviors
    B. punishment for undesirable responses
    C. reinforcing latency behaviors
    D. pairing an automatic response with a neutral stimulus

17. When children watch a model behaving in a particular
    way, their behaviors will _____.
    A. become fixated
    B. be the same as the model's
    C. be unaffected because their memories are short
    D. depend on what they saw happen to the model as a
       result of the behavior

18. The concepts of _____ theory lie between those of learning
    theory and cognitive theory.
    A. latent cognitive   C. social cognitive
    B. cognitive adaptive   D. innate cognitive

19. _____ is the principle that the amount of something does not change merely because its shape has changed.
    A. Adaption   C. Conservation
    B. Biogenetic   D. Decentering

20. In my job I care for a retarded child who seems not to remember when objects disappear from her sight. I can conclude that some aspects of her impairment place her cognitively below the level of a _____ -old child.
    A. one month
    B. six month
    C. nine month
    D. one year

21. According to Case's theory of cognitive and emotional development, a baby learns to show anger when _____.
    A. it can anticipate a negative stimulus
    B. it has learned to accomplish a goal and that action is interfered with
    C. it can conceptualize social injustice
    D. its schemes consolidate

22. Ethology is the study of _____.
    A. instincts   B. ethics   C. stages   D. extinction

23. If a teenager is in trouble and is claiming his genes "made him do it," he had better hope his parents are _____.
    A. psychoanalysts   C. behaviorists
    B. cognitive therapists   D. sociobiologists

24. Bob gives his dog a doggie treat each time the dog is a little more successful at standing on his hind legs. Bob is engaging in a(n) _____ procedure.
    A. autonomy   C. extinction
    B. shaping   D. preformation

25. Watson's famous experiment with "little Albert" was _____ conditioning.
    A. extraneous   C. classical
    B. operant   D. cognitive

26. Mary's therapist is curing her phobia of beetles by deconditioning. Mary is probably _____.
    A. getting a large container of live beetles dumped in her lap while the therapist records her brain waves and muscle tension signals
    B. being slowly introduced to small harmless beetles
    C. watching her best friend play with a beetle
    D. having to keep a diary of all the thoughts and feelings she has about beetles

27. According to Kohlberg's theory, a child who is in the
    _____stage of the _____ level will make moral decisions
    based on avoiding punishment.
    A. third, preconventional moral reasoning
    B. first, postconventional moral reasoning
    C. second, conventional moral reasoning
    D. first, preconventional moral reasoning

28. In operant conditioning, _____.
    A. a reinforcer and an action are paired
    B. a reflex and a neutral stimulus are paired
    C. a reflex and a reinforcer are paired
    D. an action and a reflex are paired

29. If your psychology instructor says her job is to help you
    add to your "software," her approach is probably that
    of _____.
    A. information processing   C. behavior analysis
    B. social cognition   D. reaction formation

30. Case's new theory integrates _____.
    A. Piaget's theory, information processing, and emotional
       development
    B. psychoanalysis, cognition, and emotional development
    C. information processing, neobehaviorism, and
       cognition
    D. automatization, autonomy, and preparedness

THOUGHT QUESTIONS

1. What are your personal views on children? Which theory in
   this chapter is closest to your view of child development?
   Tell what part of the theory you agree with and what part
   you do not agree with and why.

2. Do you have fears? Are any of them phobias? Discuss the
   possible explanations for the phobia (someone else's if you
   don't have one). In your opinion, which explanation is
   likely to be the most accurate one?

3. If all the neighborhood cats come when you call "Here,
   kitty, kitty!" for your cat, what solution would this
   chapter suggest?

4. Who are people in your life that you know have served as
   models for you? What learning is it that you have gotten
   from watching them and their consequences? Do you serve
   as a model for anyone that you are aware of? When is the
   last time you learned something by watching a stranger's
   behavior and consequences?

ANSWERS WITH PAGE REFERENCES

Fill in the Blanks

1. preformation (79)
2. tabula rasa (79)
   nurture (79)
3. society (80)
4. Darwin (81)
5. species-specific (81)
6. psychoanalysis (81)
7. id, ego, and superego
   (82-83)
   id (82)
   ego (83)
   superego (83)
8. repressed (83)
   displaced (83)
9. four (83-85)
   oral (83)
   anal stage (83)
10. phallic (84)
    identify (84)
11. period (85)
    stage (85)
12. genital (85)
13. social interactions (85)
    eight (86)
    four (83-85)
    period (85)
    throughout life (86)
14. Classical behaviorists
    (87-88)
    Neobehaviorists (93)
    behavior analysts (93)
15. classical conditioning
    (89)
    operant conditioning (89)
16. reinforcement (89)
    punishment (92)
17. partial (90)
    extinction (90)
    continuous (91)
18. deconditioning (91)
    modeling (91)

19. learning (93)
20. Cognitive (95)
21. cognitive (95)
    his own (95)
22. learning theory (96)
    two (96)
    does (96)
    consequences (96)
    gradual (96)
    stages (96)
23. sensorimotor (97)
    object permanence (98)
    representational (98)
    egocentric (99)
24. concrete (99-100)
    formal (100)
    abstract (100)
25. Kohlberg (102)
    three (102)
    sex (103)
    significant (103)
26. selectively (102)
    acted on (102)
    stored (102)
    retrieved (102)
    acted on (102)
27. computer (104)
    inborn structural (104)
    rules or strategies (104)
28. Piaget's (104)
    information-processing
    (104)
    stages (104)
    information processing
    (104)
29. innate (106)
    ethology (106)
    sociobiology (106)
    ethology (106)
    instincts (106)
    Sociobiologists (107)
    genes (107)

Multiple Choice

1. A (78)	9. D (85)	17. D (94)	25. C (88)
2. C (108)	10. B (86)	18. C (95)	26. B (91)
3. D (80)	11. B (83)	19. C (99)	27. D (102)
4. D (81)	12. A (97)	20. C (98)	28. A (89)
5. C (82)	13. D (98)	21. B (105)	29. A (104)
6. B (83)	14. C (102)	22. A (106)	30. A (104)
7. C (84)	15. B (88)	23. D (107)	
8. B (83)	16. D (89)	24. B (92)	

SUGGESTED ANSWERS TO THOUGHT QUESTIONS

1. The following list contains some attitudes that people may
    have about children.
    a. Children should be seen and not heard.
    b. Children should be the center of family life.
    c. Children are what they live (an environmental
        viewpoint).
    d. Some children are just bad seed or born bad
        (inheritance as primary influence).

2. Some of the common phobias are snakes, spiders, and height.
    Behaviorists would say that one learns to be afraid. Some
    theorists believe that humans are genetically prepared for
    certain fears since they are learned so easily. Freud
    would say that phobias are symbolized representations of
    unconscious conflicts of a sexual or aggressive nature.

3. Place the cat in a closed area such as a room. Use
    another auditory signal to announce that food is available:
    "Come, Augustus," "Food time, Fluffy," or clang the spoon
    against the side of the can. Many cats respond to an
    electric can opener (not loud enough to summon an outdoor
    cat). Do this several times in a row so that the cat can
    pair the new auditory cue with food.

4. The following list illustrates some of the people who serve
    as models for others: parents, teachers, neighbors,
    siblings, friends, ministers, entertainment stars,
    athletes, and even occasional strangers. In watching these
    models we may behave like the model in hopes of getting a
    similar positive consequence. We may also learn not to do
    certain behaviors to avoid the negative consequences that
    the behaviors brought to others.

Chapter 4

From Conception to Birth

AN OVERVIEW OF THE CHAPTER

Chapter Four traces the development of the infant from conception through birth.

Prenatal development can be divided into three stages: the germinal stage (first two weeks), the stage of the embryo (two weeks to two months), and the stage of the fetus (two months to birth). In describing and explaining these stages, the text particularly focuses on the development of the nervous system since it is critical to all aspects of the child's future development.

There are many factors that influence prenatal development and health. Two of these, genetic and chromosomal factors, were discussed in Chapter Two. Environmental factors (teratogens) that cause abnormal prenatal development or health problems in the newborn are covered in detail in this chapter. Among these factors are diseases, drugs, hormones, cigarette smoke, alcohol, radiation, and pollutants in air or water. Some of these factors can be monitored and controlled during pregnancy to increase the likelihood of a healthy infant.

Next, the three stages of childbirth are explained. Possible complications in the birth process are described, along with the effects these complications may have on the child's later development. A variety of approaches to how the birth process should be handled are discussed.

The chapter concludes with Margaret Mead's observation that regardless of the circumstances of the delivery of the baby, the baby receives a drastic jolt as it is moved out of an environment designed for its growth and into the outer world.

KEY TERMS AND CONCEPTS

umbilical cord
placenta
uterus
neonate
prenatal period
period of gestation
conception ovary
ovum
Fallopian tubes
ovulate
artificial insemination
cervix
in vitro fertilization
surrogate mother
birth mother
legal mother
zygote
germinal stage
embryo
fetus
blastula
amnion
differentiation
cephalocaudal
proximodistal
amniotic fluid
trimester
critical period
testes
hormones
androgens
estrogens
nervous system
central nervous system

sensory nerve
motor nerve
neuron
synapse
cortex
reflex
cross the placenta
antibodies
Rh factor
rubella
toxoplasmosis
herpes
AIDS
Pre-eclampsia
teratogen
alpha-fetoprotein test (AFP)
fetal alcohol syndrome
lightening
Braxton-Hicks contraction
dilation
transition
anoxia
breech birth
cesarean
forceps delivery
postpartum depression
small for gestational age
   (SGA)
Lamaze method
psychoprophylactic method
Leboyer method
birthing center
birthing chair

CHAPTER OBJECTIVES--CHECK YOURSELF
By the time you've finished reading and studying this chapter,
you should be able to:

1. Detail the sequence of events that leads to conception.

2. Discuss the level of infertility in the U.S. today, and
    list the possible causes for this phenomenon.

3. List four alternative paths to parenthood.

4. List the three stages of prenatal development.

5. Explain how a fetus becomes a boy or a girl, and what the
    statistics are for the occurrence of each.

6. Describe the support structures that provide for the infant's prenatal environment.

7. Explain how identical twins develop, and in which prenatal stage the process occurs.

8. Explain the two patterns of growth that are seen in prenatal development.

9. Explain the difference between "stages of prenatal development" and "stages of pregnancy."

10. Explain the concept of a "critical period."

11. Describe fetal behaviors in utero.

12. Explain the current critical limits of survival for a fetus.

13. Give a brief summary of the development (prenatal through a year after birth) of the nervous system.

14. Explain how substances get to the baby through the mother.

15. List substances that are known to cross from mother to child and the effect of each on the embryo/fetus.

16. List possible complications of childbirth and the effects each can have on the fetus.

17. Explain postpartum depression.

18. Describe alternative styles of birthing and the purpose each serves.

19. Explain the three classes of birth defects and give examples of each type.

20. Explain the health implications for low-birthweight babies.

HELPFUL HINTS

1. Ask to what extent you need to know bodily dimensions throughout prenatal development.

2. Draw pictures of the various stages of development. The mental and physical effort put into making the drawings (whether they are good or not), may well translate into extra points for you, since working more actively with the concepts will probably enhance your retention of the material. If a picture is worth a thousand words, see if it is worth five or ten more points on your test grade, too.

3. If a movie of prenatal development is not part of your instructor's class presentation, go to your college library to view one.

REVIEW EXERCISE--FILL IN THE BLANKS

1. The prenatal period begins at the moment of _____. The prenatal period is also called the period of _____. It begins in the _____ of the mother.

2. The small clump of dividing cells embeds itself in the soft lining of the _____. The _____ is the large organ that is responsible for collecting nutrients for the fetus.

3. "Test tube" fertilization, where egg and sperm meet in a glass laboratory dish is called _____.

4. The fertilized human egg is called the _____. For the first two months after conception, the growing organism is called a(n) _____. From two months after conception until birth, the organism is called a(n) _____.

5. _____ are biochemical substances that are present in the blood in very small amounts. They determine what kind of sex organs the fetus will develop. The testes secrete the male hormone, called _____. Ovaries secrete the female hormones, called _____. All fetuses begin with the same undifferentiated sex. Unless androgens are present a _____ sexed body will develop.

6. Slightly more than half of American births are _____ babies.

7. The basic cell of the nervous system is the _____. These cells communicate with one another across gaps called _____. _____ neurons carry messages to the central nervous system to provide the brain with information about the external world or the internal world of the body. _____ neurons carry messages from the central nervous system to the muscles, telling them to do something, either contract or relax.

8. Babies are born with simple automatic responses called _____.

9. The _____ of the brain, which most differentiates us from lower animals, allows us to speak, to think, to plan, and even to laugh.

10. Substances that can be transmitted from the mother to the embryo or fetus are said to _____.

11. When the mother's blood type is Rh negative and the baby's is Rh positive, the mother's body may form _____ that attack and destroy the baby's blood cells.

12. An environmental factor capable of producing abnormalities in a developing embryo or fetus is called a _____.

13. A preganant woman who drinks two to four ounces of alcohol a day runs a sizable risk of giving birth to an infant with _____.

14. A woman who smokes gives birth to a baby that weighs, on the average, _____ less than those of nonsmoking mothers.

15. The first stage of labor is called _____; this refers to the process of the opening up of the _____. The _____ happens at the end of the second stage of labor, called _____. During the third stage of labor the _____ is expelled.

16. _____, which is an oxygen deficit to the fetus, may occur prenatally if the mother is anemic, takes certain drugs, smokes cigarettes, or drinks alcohol. It may happen during the birth process if the fetus' _____ to the mother via the _____ is impaired.

17. Premature birth is defined as delivery _____ weeks or more before the due date, which should be _____ after conception. The limit on survival for a "preemie" at this point in medical technology is _____ months premature.

18. American babies weigh about _____ pounds at birth. Those that are less than 5 1/2 pounds, although they may be full-term or nearly full-term, are called _____.

19. In a _____ birth, the room is dimly lit and noise is kept to a minimum. Another alternative for birthing is to use a facility that may or may not be part of a hospital. These _____ are more relaxed and homelike, and family and friends are welcome. Sometimes a _____ is used which allows a woman to sit upright so that gravity facilitates the birth.

PRACTICE EXAM

1. The prenatal period is _____.
   A. the first two weeks after conception
   B. after the embryonic period and before the fetal period
   C. from conception to birth
   D. the most crucial for learning to breathe

2. Conception normally takes place in the _____.
   A. uterus   C. Fallopian tubes
   B. vagina   D. ovaries

3. Implantation occurs in the _____.
   A. uterus   C. Fallopian tubes
   B. vagina   D. cervix

4. Which of the following is <u>not</u> a prenatal stage of development?
   A. fetal stage   C. germinal stage
   B. embryonic stage   D. fallopian stage

5. During differentiation, the nervous system develops out of the _____ layer.
   A. inner   B. middle   C. outer   D. amnion

6. During the stage of the embryo, _____.
   A. growth is very rapid.
   B. growth is fastest at the outer and lower parts of the body
   C. the embryo lengthens to about twenty inches
   D. the embryo is attached in the fallopian wall

7. Identical twins form during _____; fraternal twins form during _____.
   A. the surrogate stage; the germinal stage
   B. the embryonic stage; the insemination stage
   C. the germinal stage; conception
   D. the fetal stage; differentiation

8. Androgens _____.
   A. cause the vagina to form
   B. cause the penis to form
   C. determine brain size
   D. regulate metabolism of nutrients

9. Because of the _____ growth pattern, problems late in the embryonic stage are likely to be problems with the hands and feet.
   A. proximodistal   C. cephalocaudal
   B. alpha-fetal   D. modal

10. Your friend is upset because her physician said she had now entered the third stage of prenatal development. She did not think she was anywhere near six months pregnant yet. Her problem probably is _____.
    A. postpartum depression
    B. pre-eclamptic anxiety
    C. confusion about the terms "stages of pregnancy" and "stages of prenatal development"
    D. that she is lacking an emotional support network including that of her physician

11. A woman who has very irregular menstrual cycles, has had a positive pregnancy test. She has no idea when her baby is due. After she reported feeling the baby move in early January, a knowledgeable friend tells her the baby will probably be born in _____.
   A. February
   B. April
   C. June
   D. August

12. The placenta _____.
   A. manufactures nutrients for the fetus
   B. mixes maternal and fetal blood for nutrient exchange
   C. is the support structure that can receive some molecules and organisms from the mother
   D. protects the fetus from all harmful circumstances

13. Any environmental factor that can cause abnormalities in the developing embryo or fetus is called a _____.
   A. rubella   C. toxemia
   B. teratogen   D. defect

14. If the fetus produces no sex hormones at all, it will develop _____.
   A. female organs   C. both sets of sex organs
   B. male organs   D. neither set of sex organs

15. You overhear a woman say she is sure she had experienced "lightening" that morning. You can conclude that she probably _____.
   A. has conceived during the previous month's ovulation
   B. felt the baby move into the third trimester
   C. is about a month from delivery of her first child
   D. has been practicing doing Braxton-Hicks contractions at her Lamaze class

16. The devastating physical side effects of DES use has been on the _____.
   A. women who used the drug themselves
   B. sexual partners of the women who used the drug
   C. daughters of DES users
   D. sons of DES users

17. If a child has severe fetal alcohol syndrome, one could conclude that the mother was definitely consuming alcohol _____.
   A. just prior to conception
   B. during implantation
   C. during the first trimester
   D. at the onset of labor

18. Labor is divided into _____ stages.
   A. 2   B. 3   C. 4   D. 5

19. During the first stage of labor _____.
    A. the cervix dilates
    B. the Fallopian tubes contract
    C. the placenta is expelled
    D. the Apgar test is administered

20. Breech birth is when a baby emerges _____.
    A. head first
    B. feet or buttocks first
    C. through the vagina
    D. through the cervix

21. Anoxia may occur as a result of _____.
    A. the mother's anemia
    B. a restricted flow problem in the umbilical cord
    C. the mother's smoking during pregnancy
    D. all of the above

22. The average weight of an infant at birth is _____
    pounds.
    A. 3   B. 5   C. 7   D. 9

23. The Lamaze method of childbirth _____.
    A. eases delivery by improved techniques in the use of
       pain killing medications
    B. involves training the mother and father (or emotional
       support person) for active participation in childbirth
    C. reduces the length of labor
    D. uses hypnosis

24. Although in our culture, people do not want wrinkles on
    their faces, they definitely should want them on _____.
    A. the cortex of their brains
    B. their internal sex organs
    C. their chromosomes
    D. their newborns

25. Toxemia is associated with _____.
    A. viruses   C. low blood pressure
    B. microorganisms   D. high blood pressure

26. Fetal alcohol syndrome can involve _____.
    A. mental retardation
    B. growth deficiencies
    C. abnormalities of the head and face
    D. all of the above

27. Most cases of low birth weight are due to _____.
    A. poor nutrition   C. fetal alcohol syndrome
    B. premature birth   D. genetic abnormality

28. Ironically, the only woman in your whole family who
    had trouble becoming pregnant was the one who appeared
    to be the healthiest and most physically fit. Her problem
    might have been that _____.
    A. she used too much energy on exercise and had intercourse
       too infrequently
    B. she was too thin
    C. she had overdosed on vitamins too frequently to ovulate
       regularly
    D. she was a vegetarian

29. A woman who has severely scarred Fallopian tubes may have
    to consider _____ as an alternative means to parenthood.
    A. artificial insemination   C. amnion transplant
    B. in vitro fertilization   D. estrogen therapy

30. A pregnancy has ended spontaneously about six weeks after
    conception.
    A. The sex of the embryo was not apparent yet.
    B. The embryo's genetic code was not yet established.
    C. Differentiation had just begun.
    D. The placenta had not started to form yet.

THOUGHT QUESTIONS

1. If you were trying to plan a pregnancy to insure (as much
   as is possible) a healthy baby, what are some of your
   considerations?

2. What personal activities might you avoid during pregnancy
   that you might otherwise engage in?

3. Make a list of characteristics that would be observed in a
   neonate.

4. A great controversy in our society today centers around the
   question, "when does human life begin?" After studying
   this chapter, what do you say? Defend your answer from
   material in your text.

ANSWERS WITH PAGE REFERENCES

Multiple Choice

1. conception (113)   4. zygote (116)
   gestation (113)   embryo (116)
   Fallopian tubes (114)   fetus (116)
2. uterus (116)   5. hormones (120)
   placenta (124)   androgens (120)
3. in vitro (115)   estrogen (120)
                               female (120)

6. male (120)
7. neuron (121)
   synapses (121)
   sensory (121)
   motor (121)
8. reflexes (122)
9. cortex (122)
10. cross the placenta (124)
11. antibodies (124)
12. teratogen (127)
13. FAS (fetal alcohol
    syndrome) (130)
14. one-half pound (132)
15. dilation (138)
    cervix (138)
    birth (139)
    transition (139)
    placenta (139)

16. anoxia (139)
    connection (139)
    umbilical cord (139)
17. three (140)
    38 (113)
    three (140-41)
18. seven (140)
    SGA (small for ges-
    tational age) (140)
19. Leboyer (143)
    birthing center (144)
    birthing chair (144)

Multiple Choice

1.	C (113)	9.	A (117)	17.	C (130)	25.	D (126)
2.	C (114)	10.	C (118)	18.	B (139)	26.	D (130)
3.	A (116)	11.	C (118)	19.	A (138)	27.	B (140)
4.	D (116)	12.	C (124)	20.	B (139)	28.	B (114)
5.	C (117)	13.	B (127)	21.	D (139)	29.	B (115)
6.	A (117)	14.	A (120)	22.	C (140)	30.	A (120)
7.	C (116)	15.	C (136)	23.	B (143)		
8.	B (120)	16.	C (129)	24.	A (122)		

SUGGESTED ANSWERS TO THOUGHT QUESTIONS

1. You might want to consider some of the following issues:
   * Age of the mother and age of the father
   * Rh factors of mother and father
   * Health of mother, with no untreated syphilis; should
     have had rubella or an inoculation against it
   * The mother should have a nutritionally balanced diet
   * She should have regular medical attention from the
     start of the pregnancy, even a preconception checkup
   * Arrange life circumstances to reduce stress on mother
     and her emotional support system
   * Education and exercise to prepare the mother optimally
     for the delivery process

2. A prospective mother should:
   * Avoid going into situations where there are likely to
     be infectious diseases (beware of children's groups
     where they bring in everything that is going around).
   * Avoid getting a cat or cleaning the litter box.
   * Avoid eating raw beef.
   * Avoid drinking alcohol, even in moderation.

44

* Avoid taking any medications except those essential for the mother's health and approved by her physician.
* Reduce caffeine intake to less than 2-4 cups a day, and check to see what soft drinks contain caffeine.
* Avoid cigarette smoke situations.
* Avoid eating fish from areas known to be high in PCB's.
* Avoid exposure to lead based paints; do not help with the scraping down of any paint surface that contains very old paint.
* Drink bottled water if there is reason to believe that the water source may have lead from the pipes.
* Avoid spending time where one is exposed to a lot of car exhaust (freeway, large cities, working around automobiles that have their engines on).

3. The typical baby weighs about 7 pounds, has a temporarily elongated head, has a quite small chin, appears to have no neck, has a stub of the umbilical cord healing, can see and hear, and makes at least simple responses to the environment (reflexes).

4. Several possible viewpoints are that human life begins at:
    * Conception—when the individual's unique genetic code is established
    * 24 weeks after conception—fetus has some small chance of surviving on its own even though lungs and kidneys are not mature
    * 7-month fetus—when the brain develops wrinkling of the cortex which allows for the special human abilities to talk, think, and laugh
    * at birth—when the umbilical cord is cut and the baby is no longer drawing the essentials for life from the mother

Chapter 5

The Baby

AN OVERVIEW OF THE CHAPTER

Chapter Five is about babyhood. A newborn baby is called a
neonate. Research on the neonate has been very active and
productive in the last 15 years. In this chapter we will study
the characteristics of the newborn baby, the perceptual world of
the infant, and the newborn's motor development. We will also
look at physical growth from infancy to toddlerhood.

A newborn does not look like the smooth, dimpled baby shown
in the diaper commercials. The physical condition of a neonate
is rated at birth with a process called the Apgar test. A low
Apgar score indicates that the baby has less chance of
surviving.

A baby's behavior goes through different states in the
course of a day. These states are quiet and active sleep,
drowsiness, quiet and active (fussing) alertness, and crying.
Babies vary enormously in how much they cry.

Babies are born with a number of reflexes. Many of these
are essential for life. Newborns also have a number of
apparently "useless" reflexes. These reflexes disappear in
short period of time. Another behavior which disappears in a
short time is the ability, under certain conditions, to imitate
adults' facial movements.

The perceptual world of the infant has been studied by
psychologists for over 100 years. What are newborns able to
see, hear, smell, taste and feel? How do their sensory
capacities develop during infancy? Modern methods of studying
perceptual development show that the infant is much more capable
of perceiving things than previously thought.

Among the most striking changes that occur during the first
two years of the child's life are changes in motor abilities.
Your textbook points out that the newborn can do little in this
area. The head, however, is the most sophisticated. In
general, motor development proceeds from the top down and from
the center out.

The final section of this chapter deals with physical growth from infancy to toddlerhood. Size at birth is not highly correlated with size at maturity. But, height at age two is highly correlated with adult height. Brain size and growth as well as changes in body proportions are reported. A special section deals with Sudden Infant Death Syndrome (SIDS). This baby killer claims an estimated 1 out of 500 babies, most often when they are 2 or 3 months old, and usually when they are asleep.

KEY TERMS AND CONCEPTS

vernix
lanugo
Apgar test
active sleep
REM sleep
state
quiet alertness
rooting
Babinski reflex
Moro Reflex
swimming reflex
grasp reflex
walking reflex
stepping reflex
preferential-looking
technique
habituation technique
habituate
retina
depth perception

stereoscopic vision
binocular cells
visual cliff
plasticity
stereoblind
amblyopia
intermodal perception
skin senses
proprioception
kinesthesis
maturation
visual-motor skill
eye-hand coordination
visual feedback
sudden infant death syndrome
  (SIDS)
myelination
myelin
glial cell

CHAPTER OBJECTIVES--CHECK YOURSELF
By the time you've finished reading and studying this chapter, you should be able to:

1. Describe a newborn's appearance within the first minute after birth. Then explain how the Apgar Test is used to assess this neonate.

2. List and categorize the six states of sleep and wakefulness.

3. List the reflexes that a newborn has at birth. Prioritize them for importance and indicate which ones disappear.

4. List and describe the research methods used to study the perceptual abilities of babies.

5. Describe the growth and development of the baby's visual system. Include acuity levels, color detection, infant preferences in color and design, depth perception, object perception tracking, focusing, and stereoscopic vision.

6. Explain the advantages and disadvantages of plasticity.

7. Give details of the infant's auditory development.

8. Describe the infant's senses of taste and smell.

9. List the four senses that are collectively known as the skin senses.

10. Describe motor development in the infant.

11. Describe the development of visual—motor coordination.

12. Explain the recent research which shows that babies have intermodal perception.

13. Describe the physical growth pattern from birth through toddlerhood. Include gender differences and mention the brain specifically.

14. Describe the facial proportions of an infant and explain how those proportions may help insure its survival.

15. State the statistics on SIDS, ages when SIDS is most likely to happen, and some of the hypothesized causes.

HELPFUL HINT

Ask your instructor how much detail you should know on an infant's color discrimination.

REVIEW EXERCISE--FILL IN THE BLANKS

1. _____ is a fatty substance that protects the skin of the fetus in the uterus and helps to grease his passage down the birth canal. _____ is fine hair that covers the fetus at birth and will soon fall out. The _____ test rates breathing, muscle tone, heart rate, response to an irritating stimulus, and pinkness of skin soon after birth.

2. In _____ sleep, also known as _____, which stands for _____, the eyes can be seen moving beneath the closed lids. The newborn spends _____ of his sleep time in this type of sleep while an adult spends _____ of his sleep time in this state.

3. A touch of a stimulus on the cheek of an infant causes him to exhibit the _____ reflex, a turning of his head toward the stimulus. The _____ reflex is the baby's startle response to a loud noise or a sudden loss of support.

4. It is easy to tell when infants are cold because first they turn pale and the then they turn _____. Babies have more sensitivity to cold than adults because they lack the layer of _____ that helps to insulate the bodies of adults, and their bodies are _____ in mass than the adults.

5. In the 1950's Fantz developed the _____ technique to determine whether babies would look at certain kinds of pictures more than others. The _____ technique allows researchers to study the infant's ability to make visual discriminations. The _____ was developed to study the depth perception of young animals. A measure of _____ is sometimes used to indicate the infant is experiencing fear.

6. The essential parts of the eye are complete by _____ after conception. A newborn can best see objects that are about _____ from his face. By age _____, the infant's vision is near adult level. Generally, babies of all ages decidedly prefer to look at moderately _____ patterns.

7. There are specialized neurons in the brain called _____ cells, that receive inputs from both the left eye and the right eye. These are responsible for _____ vision, which is one of the major factors in _____ perception.

8. The structure of the nervous system is not entirely determined in advance; there is a certain amount of flexibility, or what neurologists call _____.

9. Hubel and Wiesel found that an animal's visual system could be permanently impaired if one of its eyes was kept closed for a period of time _____ in life after _____. For this reason, crossed eyes should be corrected by about _____ of age. If early correction is not made, _____ vision may be lost permanently. Also the child may develop _____ (also known as "_____,") which is blindness at the brain level even though the eye itself is perfectly normal.

10. Although a fetus has no opportunity to use its eyes before birth, its ears have already been functioning for _____. Very young babies seem to be particularly attuned to the sounds of _____. Apparently young babies can _____ some speech sounds that _____ cannot.

11. Babies demonstrate _____ perception very early by showing distress when the "wrong" voices seem to be coming from their mothers.

12. Because there is _____ in regard to how sensitive a newborn baby is to pain, the text authors suggest that it is best to assume that they are as sensitive as _____.

13. Sitting, crawling, and walking are _____ skills.

14. Reaching for a toy and drawing a circle are examples of _____ skills. Seeing the visible results of what happens when you direct a muscle to contract is called _____. Normal human infants learn how to reach accurately for objects by the time they are about _____ months old.

15. Motor development starts at the _____(top/bottom). It proceeds from the center to the _____. Many studies on Hopi infants and American twins imply that motor milestones occur at a certain stage of physical development and that _____ does not matter very much except under conditions of extreme _____. If that is the case, then that development is purely a factor of _____. However, Zelazo demonstrated that _____ could help maintain the walking reflex. The babies that had this experience walked _____ earlier. Whether early walking is advantageous or not is still unclear.

16. The leading killer of babies between one month and twelve months of age is _____, with the age of most frequent occurrence being _____. Because autopsies reveal symptoms similar to suffocation, attention has been focused on failure of the _____ system as a possible cause.

17. During the first year, the average newborn will grow about _____ inches and _____ pounds. Size at birth _____ (does/does not) correlate with size at maturity. The best indicator of adult size of an infant is the size of his _____.

18. Almost all of the cells in our body continue to divide after birth, except for the _____. After birth they increase in _____, not number.

19. In addition to the increase in the size of neurons, the brain increases in size by a factor of _____ from birth to adulthood because of developing deposits of a fatty coating called _____ on nerve cells, and to the increase in the number of _____ cells which support and nourish neurons.

20. The newborn is not just smaller than an adult; his body _____ are different. Konrad Lorenz, has proposed a theory that the different appearance of the head and body of young animals "triggers" a(n) _____ response in older animals of the species. Girls seem to develop this response at about age _____ years, and boys at about _____ years.

PRACTICE EXAM

1. The fatty substance that protects the fetus in utero and that helps grease the passage down the birth canal is called the _____.
   A. lanugo   B. myelin   C. vernix   D. glial cells

2. The Apgar test measures, among other things, _____.
   A. the strength of the baby's apgar reflex
   B. oxygen in the delivery room
   C. heart rate of the newborn
   D. temperature of the newborn

3. The newborn _____.
   A. has very similar sleep cycles to an adult, although the baby sleeps much longer
   B. sleeps much more deeply than the adult
   C. spends half of his sleep in "active" sleep
   D. is in coma during part of its sleep cycle

4. The reflex in which an infant turns his head toward something that has touched his cheek is called the _____ reflex.
   A. rooting   B. Babinski   C. Moro   D. tonic neck

5. The _____ reflex is a "startle response" to a loud noise or other stimulus.
   A. Moro   B. Babinski   C. apgar   D. grasp

6. When a baby habituates to a stimulus, _____.
   A. the baby is displaying a memory for that stimulus
   B. the baby prefers it to all new stimuli
   C. the stimulus arouses full attention and interest
   D. the baby will seek that stimulus out of habit

7. The visual cliff apparatus was important because it tested _____.
   A. visual acuity of neonates
   B. depth perception
   C. for amblyopia to prevent stereoblindness
   D. object perception

8. Studies on the importance of early visual experiences have shown that _____.
   A. experiences partially determine which neurons and neural connections are kept and developed and which are discarded
   B. the structure of the nervous system is entirely determined at birth when the baby starts to breathe on its own
   C. the plasticity theory of neurons should be discarded
   D. amblyopia is due to intermodal kinesthetics

9. Your year-old toddler gives evidence that he cannot see
    across a ten-foot room. You should ____.
    A. not worry; adult quality of vision is not reached until
       age five years
    B. try to clear vernix that may still remain in his eyes
    C. take him to a physician that specializes in the care
       of children's eye problems
    D. get his eyes checked for glasses before he starts school

10. According to research, nursery decor should be _____
    to give optimal visual stimulation to the baby.
    A. a bright intense solid color
    B. pink or blue depending on the child's sex
    C. quarter inch stripes of pastel colors
    D. moderately complex patterns in black and white

11. A baby can first make eye contact at about age _____.
    A. 12 hours   B. one week   C. 6 weeks   D. 6 months

12. For a baby to be able to see stereoscopically, it must
    _____.
    A. be able to coordinate its two eyes
    B. be able to see lines a quarter inch in width
    C. have had practice on the visual cliff
    D. have been born prematurely

13. Plasticity of neuron development allows _____.
    A. adjustment for skull size
    B. adjustment to size of the mother's pelvis for birth
    C. adjustment to environmental demands
    D. adjustment for proprioception

14. Amblyopia is ultimately the result of a problem in the
    _____.
    A. retina   B. apgar   C. amnion   D. brain

15. Crossed eyes should be corrected by age _____.
    A. two weeks   C. one year
    B. two months   D. six years

16. The ability to overcome a brain injury is based on _____.
    A. proprioception   C. SIDS
    B. anoxia   D. plasticity

17. A friend thinks her baby formula may have spoiled. Concluding that the infant will not drink the formula if it does not taste right, she decides to give it to the infant anyway. She is wrong because _____.
   A. babies do not have taste sensations until they are 12 weeks old
   B. a hungry baby cannot make taste discriminations; this prevents them from starving because of picky eating habits
   C. babies have such a strong sucking reflex that they may be unable to stop sucking even though they may recognize that the taste is bad
   D. baby bottle nipples reach the back of the tongue where there are no taste buds

18. In general, motor development starts _____.
   A. at the extremities and works inward
   B. at the top and works its way down
   C. with the simple and precise and moves to the general
   D. with the small muscles and proceeds to the large ones

19. Development that is due to carrying out of plans preprogrammed in the genes and not to the child's actions or experiences is called _____.
   A. cephalocaudal   C. myelination
   B. kinesthesis   D. maturation

20. Visual-motor skills _____.
   A. include walking, sitting, and crawling
   B. are also called eye-hand coordination
   C. are perfected during the first months of life
   D. will develop normally, regardless of experience

21. SIDS _____.
   A. is caused by a defect in the part of the brain that controls breathing
   B. is most common between 9 and 12 months of age
   C. babies have numerous symptoms of illness before they die
   D. may be related to respiratory problems

22. By two years of age, _____.
   A. a boy has achieved about half of his adult height
   B. a girl has already achieved more than half of her adult height
   C. girls are more physically mature than boys
   D. all of the above

23. The number of neurons in our brains _____.
   A. at birth is virtually the same as in adulthood
   B. continues to increase until two years of age
   C. is half the adult number
   D. is twice as large as the adult number

24. Konrad Lorenz, a biologist, believes that _____.
    A. parents of young animals must learn to respond to their
       infants
    B. nurturing instincts are specific to females
    C. babyish features of young animals are the result of
       fetal brain growth
    D. nurturing impulses are triggered by the babyish features
       of young animals

25. A young mother reports that her six-week-old baby hates
    shoes. She says every time she tries to put shoes on him
    he fans his toes out so that it is hard to get his toes
    into the shoes. What the mother is seeing is _____.
    A. evidence of stereoscopic development
    B. the first signs of a strong-willed child
    C. a Babinski reflex
    D. intermodal perception

26. The preferential-looking technique of Fantz showed that
    given two different pictures, most babies usually _____.
    A. look at each of two pictures for approximately equal
       periods of time
    B. seem to "like" one picture more than the other
    C. tend to look at the picture on the right
    D. are unable to tell the difference between two pictures

27. Babies can hear from _____.
    A. the time of conception
    B. when the embryo becomes a fetus
    C. about six months after conception
    D. birth

28. The ability to recognize that certain sights and certain
    sounds are related is called _____.
    A. proprioception
    B. cephalocaudal perception
    C. intermodal perception
    D. intramodal perception

29. The sense that tells you the direction and speed of the
    movements of your own body is called _____.
    A. maturation   C. preformation
    B. kinesthesis   D. myelination

30. As a student buys two candy bars, he says to his friend "I
    was born liking sweets."
    A. The student's statement has no basis in research data.
    B. The student's statement is true only if he is an insulin
       dependent diabetic.
    C. The student's statement is true.
    D. He is wrong. Babies do not like sweets at all; their
       preference is for salty tasting items.

THOUGHT QUESTIONS

1. In Chapter Four you were ask to make a list of characteristics that would be observed in a neonate. After having studied Chapter Five, add to that list.

2. What is a possible explanation for two reflexes (imitating facial smiles and localization of sounds) that are present at birth, disappear a short time later, and then within a few months reappear as learned behaviors?

3. What are some further implications of neonates' preferences for stories that their mothers read aloud to them while they were in utero?

4. Girls, on the average, proceed at a maturation rate faster than boys. What are some advantages and disadvantages of this gender difference?

ANSWERS WITH PAGE REFERENCES

Fill in the Blanks

1. vernix (149)
   lanugo (149)
   Apgar (149)
2. active (149)
   REM (149)
   rapid eye movement (149)
   half (150)
   a quarter (150)
3. rooting (153)
   Moro (154)
4. blue (153)
   fat (153)
   much smaller (153)
5. preferential-looking
      (158)
   habituation (158)
   visual cliff (162)
   heart rate (162)
6. seven months (157)
   8-12 inches (157)
   6-8 months (157)
   complex (157)
7. binocular (160)
   stereoscopic (160)
   depth (160)
8. plasticity (163)

9. early (163)
   birth (163)
   one year (163)
   stereoscopic (163)
   amblyopia (163)
   lazy eye (163)
10. 3 months (164)
    human speech (165)
    discriminate (165)
    adults (165)
11. intermodal (166)
12. controversy (168)
    other people (169)
13. motor (169)
14. visual motor (172)
    visual feedback (173)
    5-6 (172)
15. top (169)
    extremities (169)
    experience (171)
    deprivation (171)
    maturation (171)
    practice (171)
    a few weeks (171)
16. SIDS (174)
    2-3 months (175)
    respiratory (175)

17. 10 (175)
     15 (175)
     does not (175)
     parents (176)
18. neurons (176)
     size (176)

19. four (176)
     myelin (176)
     glial (176)
20. proportions (177)
     nurturing (178)
     12-13 (178)
     17 (178)

Multiple Choice

1.	C (149)	9.	C (157)	17.	C (167)	25.	C (154)
2.	C (149)	10.	D (157)	18.	B (169)	26.	B (158)
3.	C (150)	11.	C (160)	19.	D (170)	27.	C (164)
4.	A (153)	12.	A (161)	20.	B (172)	28.	C (166)
5.	A (154)	13.	C (163)	21.	D (174)	29.	B (168)
6.	A (158)	14.	D (163)	22.	D (176)	30.	C (167)
7.	B (162)	15.	C (163)	23.	A (176)		
8.	A (163)	16.	D (163)	24.	D (178)		

SUGGESTED ANSWERS TO THOUGHT QUESTIONS

1. Neonates can localize and even imitate adult facial
    expressions. She recognizes her mother's voice and can
    even demonstrate a preference for hearing a particular
    story that she heard while in utero. Even a newborn has a
    tendency to associate her concurrent visual and auditory
    experiences.

2. Perhaps these are vestigial reflexes for some past survival
    circumstance (to keep from getting tossed out of the cave
    by frustrated parents). Or perhaps the existence of these
    reflexes allows the neonate some early practice in
    responding to his environment. The practice of these
    behaviors may affect the pruning and shaping of neural
    connections. Perhaps if the child did not have these
    reflexes, by the time he could have learned the behaviors
    purely from experience, the timing would be too late and
    valuable neural formatting would have already been done.

3. Newborns demonstrating a preference for stories their
    mothers read to them while they were still in utero not
    only indicates they have working hearing before they are
    born, but also working memory. While they certainly have
    no knowledge of the meaning of their memories, they may
    have the ability to recognize tonal patterns and verbal
    sequences. And while it may seem farfetched, this might
    incline one to be careful about loud negative emotional
    outbursts during the later stages of pregnancy.

4. An advantage of early maturation for any organism is that it will have more advanced skills for survival than its late maturing peers. A possible disadvantage is that the more mature organism may not have some other skills needed to allow safe use of its advantage. Your text explained this in connection with early walking. Another possible disadvantage is that early development, particularly in utero, may not allow the early maturer as much neural shaping and pruning through interaction with the environment to produce optimal neural function. In other words, lack of development may correlate with plasticity of neuron function.

Chapter 6

The First Social Relationships

AN OVERVIEW OF THE CHAPTER

The first social relationships for babies are usually with
their parents. Much of this chapter will focus on the
relationships between mothers and babies because women are the
primary caregivers in all known cultures. In our culture, a
growing number of fathers are taking a more active parenting
role. However, such families are still in the minority.

Newborn babies are not very sociable. However, as early as
four weeks, they respond differently to a person than to an
object. Babies begin to make eye contact and start smiling at
people when they are about 6 or 7 weeks old. Their
responsiveness suggests that they are reinforced by people
responding to them. By being able to influence the behavior of
the people around them, they are learning to have an effect on
the world they live in.

Some babies are better than others at communicating their
needs to their parents and at rewarding their parents for
responding. It is clear that from birth babies differ in the
way they respond to people and to situations. Some babies are
born "easy babies" and some are born "difficult babies" with
many in between. Babies also differ from birth in how much they
like to be cuddled. These differences can affect how a mother
or father responds to the baby. This is important because the
way the parents respond to a baby can be critical to the baby's
social development. Parents who respond quickly and
consistently to babies' cries produce babies who cry very
little. Babies who are completely ignored also end up crying
very little, but they may never form what Erikson calls "basic
trust." Parents who respond slowly or inconsistently to babies
cries produce babies who cry the most.

Parents are not all alike, either. Parents treat male and
female infants differently, even though sex differences in
infancy are negligible. Fathers tend to pay less attention to
their babies than do mothers. Fathers are more likely to pick

up a child for play, while mothers are more likely to pick up a
child for caregiving. Fathers' play is more physical and less
verbal than mothers' play.

     Attachment is an emotional tie that develops between the
child and his/her parents, usually between 6 and 9 months of
age. Babies show separation distress when a person to whom they
are attached leaves them alone in an unfamiliar place. Fear of
strangers appears at about this same time. When they are under
stress, babies are more likely to turn to their mothers.
However, in the United States, most boys seem to prefer their
fathers to their mothers by the time they are two years of age.
If a father does little or no caregiving, his baby is less
likely to become attached to him. Children without parents can
also form attachments--usually to whoever is the primary
caregiver. If no caring adults are present, a child can form an
attachment to other children. The general quality of the baby's
interactions with another person seems to be the ultimate
factor in determining whether an attachment will form. Failure
to form any attachments, as might happen in an institution where
there are many transient caregivers, can have serious
consequences for the child's social and emotional development.
Children who have no opportunity to form attachments before the
age of 4 may be unable to form deep and lasting relationships
with anyone.

     Toddlerhood begins in the child's second year of life, The
toddler struggles for autonomy or self determination. This is
also a time when socialization begins in earnest--a time when
the child must learn the attitudes, behaviors, knowledge, and
skills that are necessary to get along in society. At this
point in a child's life, socialization is primarily the parents'
responsibility.

KEY TERMS AND CONCEPTS

vocalize
contingent
basic trust
learned helplessness
security object
empathy
attachment
separation distress
separation anxiety
social referencing
ethology
imprinting

sensitive period
security of attachment
securely attached
insecurely attached
Strange Situation
resistant
avoidant
bonding
toddlerhood
autonomy
socialization

CHAPTER OBJECTIVES--CHECK YOURSELF

By the time you've finished reading and studying this chapter, you should be able to:

1. Describe the progression of social behaviors from birth to 6 or 7 weeks.

2. List several ways in which adults interact differently with infants than with other adults.

3. Describe a two-month-old's play with his mother.

4. Explain how babies can know that they are having an effect on the world, and how this can influence their behavior.

5. Describe the difference between easy babies, difficult babies, and slow-to-warm-up babies.

6. Explain how cuddlers and non-cuddlers seem to be different.

7. Compare mothers' and fathers' interactions with babies.

8. Explain how the scenario of the "vanishing father" happens.

9. Describe how parents respond differently to boys and girls.

10. Compare childrearing practices in America to those of other cultures.

11. Describe an infant's ability to detect emotions and the use of this skill as part of social referencing.

12. Describe two types of attachment and describe the behaviors seen in mothers and babies for each of these types.

13. Explain why attachment develops according to the ethological perspective.

14. Discuss the development of relationships with agemates.

15. Discuss a toddler's struggle for autonomy.

16. Compare toilet training procedures among the Digo of East Africa to those typically used currently in the U.S.

REVIEW EXERCISE--FILL IN THE BLANKS

1. The research about babies' relationships has most often been about relationships between babies and their _____.

2. The newborn baby _____ (is/is not) a particularly sociable person. This may be demonstrated by the fact that eye contact does not develop until about the _____ week.

Research indicates that eye contact may be even more important than _____ in establishing the bond between parent and child.

3. When a mother talks to her baby, her rate of speech _____ and her facial expressions are _____. She is also likely to greatly _____ the length of her gazes.

4. A baby's response to a person tends to be cyclical in nature; a short period of increasing interaction followed by a short period of _____. When babies find out that they can affect the behavior of others, they are _____. _____ is usually the most effective way a baby has of getting a response from people around her.

5. By the end of the first year, a group of babies whose mothers had responded to them promptly and consistently were crying significantly _____ (more/less) than some other babies whose mothers sometimes ignored them. Babies who are usually ignored are in danger of developing what has been called _____. Babies whose cries are answered relatively quickly, and babies whose cries are not answered at all, end up crying the _____ (most/least).

6. When mothers have been intrusive and disruptive through their lack of sensitivity to baby's temperamental rhythms, baby is likely to be _____ attached and make an _____ response to her mother. As a preschooler he is likely to be more _____, _____, and less _____.

7. Babies differ from birth in the way they respond to people and to situations; these differences in styles of interaction reflect differences in _____. _____ babies are cheerful, adaptable, and regular in their habits. _____ babies are those whose biological cycles are irregular, who show negative reactions to new people or new situations, whose reactions tend to be intense, and who are often irritable or unhappy. _____ babies react negatively to anything new; but their reactions tend to be mild.

8. The quality of the relationship between parents and baby depends partly on the _____ between the baby's characteristics and the parent's expectations and attitudes.

9. In play, _____ (cuddlers/noncuddlers) did not mind being kissed, stroked or tickled, as long as they were not being held. _____ (Cuddlers/Noncuddlers) disliked being wrapped up or having their clothes put on. Schaffer and Emerson concluded that the tendency to be a cuddler or a noncuddler is _____.

10. At birth, girls are somewhat more advanced in _____ development than boys. However the differences between individual children are not as consistently seen because

the average difference between boys and girls is _____ than the differences seen _____ a group of girls or a group of boys.

11. When fathers are interacting with baby, they are more likely than mothers to be _____ baby.

12. In industrialized societies like those of North America and Western Europe, young babies sleep _____. Babies in our culture are expected to be _____ and _____.

13. The bond between a baby and his mother, developed over a period of time, is called _____. _____ is when babies cry or look unhappy when the person to whom they are attached leaves them alone in an unfamiliar place.

14. The time when attachments are formed most readily is called the _____. In humans this starts to appear about _____ months of age. This phenomenon and approximate age of onset is seen in all cultures; universal existence of this phenomenon suggests that it is _____ based. The tendency for a young animal to become attached to its mother and to remain close to her is _____; it is a survival mechanism if it keeps a baby who is developing _____ from leaving the proximity of his parents.

15. In order for a baby to form an attachment to someone, the baby has to have many opportunities to _____ with that person. A leading figure in the ethological approach to attachment, Mary Ainsworth, believes that an infant is either attached or not, and she talks about the _____ of the attachment. The quality of the attachment seems to be determined by the quality of the _____. An insensitive mother tends to end up with an _____ attached child.

16. Children adopted after age _____ may form very close attachments to their new parents, but they show the same social and emotional problems as the children who remain in institutions. Although attachments in infancy or toddlerhood are necessary for normal development, attachment to _____ may not be.

17. The study of animals' and humans' built-in patterns of behavior (sometimes called instincts) is the topic of study for the field of _____.

18. _____ means self determination or the ability to operate independently. This first becomes a major concern for the child in the _____ year of life. Ironically, this is a person whose desire is not matched by his _____. He may appear _____, thus the term "_____." The onset of this stage is probably not the time to start _____ training.

19. _____ is the learning of the attitudes, behaviors, knowledge, and skills that are necessary to get along in society. It is the primarily responsibility of the _____.

20. Critical aspects of toilet training are _____ (_____ or _____) and _____ (_____ or _____).

PRACTICE EXAM

1. Daniel Stern studied mothers' behavior with their infants and found that _____.
   A. most mothers behaved differently with babies than they would with an adult
   B. actually very few mothers used "baby talk"
   C. facial expressions made to babies were the same as those made to adults
   D. mothers' gazes at infants tended to be shorter than their gazes at adults

2. If you wanted your baby to begin making more vocalizations, a good way to increase them would be to _____.
   A. make him be quiet for long periods so he would want to make a lot of sound when given the opportunity
   B. reward sounds by responding to them in a pleasant way
   C. look the other way when the baby makes sounds
   D. frown at the baby when he is quiet

3. If a baby's cries have little effect on his caregiver's behavior, he will most likely _____.
   A. cry more and more
   B. give up and withdraw eventually
   C. develop different types of cries for different needs
   D. mature more quickly

4. Differences in the temperaments of "difficult" and "easy" babies are probably due to _____.
   A. differences in parental styles
   B. built-in differences (nature)
   C. environmental influences only
   D. levels of attachment

5. As compared to cuddlers, noncuddlers _____.
   A. tend to be firstborn
   B. tend to be famous
   C. don't like to be bounced or swung around
   D. don't like restraint of movement

6. Most of the differences between boy and girl babies _____.
   A. are small, statistically speaking, between the "average boy" and the "average girl"
   B. are extremely pronounced and important
   C. are due to the fact that at birth, boys are more advanced in physical development
   D. disappear with age, in our culture

7. American babies, as compared to babies in pre-industrial societies, are _____.
   A. more likely to sleep alone in their own rooms
   B. less likely to get attention paid to their intellectual development
   C. played with less
   D. spoken to less

8. If Jenny insists on being comforted by her mother and cries whenever her mother leaves her side, Jenny is most likely about _____.
   A. three months old
   B. one year old
   C. three years old
   D. six years old

9. The formation of attachments depends most importantly on _____.
   A. the amount of time spent with the baby in caregiving
   B. the quality of the interactions
   C. the sex of the child
   D. visual images of the parents

10. The process of imprinting is used by the _____ to illustrate that attachment is an inherited predisposition.
    A. social learning theorists
    B. Freudians
    C. ethologists
    D. Gestalt psychologists

11. What can a mother do to try to improve her relationship with her baby? She should _____.
    A. reinforce her baby for better "goodness of fit"
    B. give the baby medication to calm his temperament
    C. try to become more sensitive and responsive to the baby's signals concerning his preferences and rhythms of interaction
    D. all of the above

12. A one-year-old is going to meet his grandparents for the first time. The situation will probably be best if _____.
   A. the meeting time is during the baby's "sensitive period" during the day
   B. the child is left alone in a room and then "rescued" by his grandparents
   C. parents explain fear of strangers is universal and should be ignored
   D. introductions are made with baby in mother's arms and with mother smiling and talking to the grandparents

13. The process when a child begins to learn the attitudes, behaviors, knowledge and skills that are necessary to get along in society is called _____.
   A. attachment
   B. bonding
   C. adjustment
   D. socialization

14. Toilet training or control of elimination _____.
   A. does not exist in some societies
   B. is often gentle and late in pre-industrial societies
   C. is usually not possible until after the second birthday
   D. should be done as early as possible

15. When mothers talk to their infants, they tend to use _____.
   A. very slow speech
   B. exaggerated pitch
   C. a louder voice
   D. all of the above

16. During play with the mother, a baby may frequently need _____.
   A. a brief period without eye contact
   B. to have constant eye contact
   C. continuous, intense stimulation
   D. to see that his own actions do not change the mother's response

17. "Difficult" babies _____.
   A. result when babies' cries are repeatedly ignored
   B. are often too adaptable
   C. have irregular biological cycles
   D. are usually from single parent homes

18. Babies with security objects _____.
   A. are dealing with learned helplessness
   B. are unable to develop social referencing skills
   C. need attachment therapy
   D. are not significantly different from those who do not have them

19. Failure to form attachments will most likely result in
    _____.
    A. lower intellectual ability
    B. abnormal social development
    C. lack of temperament development
    D. rigid obedience to authority

20. The best way to deal with a "terrible two" who is
    struggling with autonomy is to _____.
    A. insist that he stay in the playpen five minutes out of
        each waking hour to teach compliance
    B. teach him short rules that he can say to himself
    C. ask him to help you with a very simple task, and be
        willing to follow his lead occasionally
    D. teach him to be contingent

21. According to research, your child might lose interest in
    her security blanket when on a family vacation if _____.
    A. she has a very frightening accident in which she
        nearly drowns
    B. her cousin teases her about being a "baby with a
        blanket"
    C. the whole family sleeps close together in a tent
    D. she stays with young cousins, none of whom has a
        security blanket

22. The period of time during which a duckling can be imprinted
    is called the _____.
    A. ethological period
    B. attachment period
    C. sensitive period
    D. critical period

23. In Ainsworth's procedure call the "Strange Situation," an
    insecurely attached child would _____.
    A. greet the mother's return with unmixed joy
    B. play happily with toys as long as the mother was there
    C. smile or babble at his mother when she returns
    D. probably greet his mother's return with a mixture of
        clinging and pushing away, angry crying, or ignoring
        her

24. In struggling for autonomy, _____.
    A. girls tend to be more rebellious than boys
    B. insecurely attached children are more obedient
    C. securely attached children are more likely to listen
        to their mother's advice
    D. unattached children are more likely to listen to their
        mother's advice with a problem they cannot solve

25. At 10 months of age, many babies _____.
    A. treat toys and other babies in the same fashion
    B. avoid eye contact with other babies
    C. greet other babies with smiles and vocalization
    D. experience stranger anxiety in response to the
        presence of another baby

26. Ethologists point out that attachments happen just when the young need it most; that is, when children _____.
   A. become mobile
   B. are fed solid food
   C. start to interact with their mothers
   D. first encounter strangers

27. As compared to mothers, fathers are more likely to _____ with their _____.
   A. watch TV; children
   B. play; sons
   C. sing; daughters
   D. teach; children

28. When babies discover they can have an impact on the behavior of others they are _____.
   A. delighted   C. terrified
   B. mildly frightened   D. perplexed (confused)

29. When mothers respond quickly and consistently to their babies' cries, their babies are likely to _____.
   A. become "difficult" children
   B. bond earlier
   C. cry less
   D. have temper tantrums

30. You are a toy manufacturer who wants to test out new toys on one-year-olds. If you want the child to be most comfortable and relaxed for the testing, you should arrange the situation such that the baby is _____.
   A. in the room alone with the toy
   B. in the room with his mother present
   C. in the room with a female stranger
   D. in the room with a male stranger

THOUGHT QUESTIONS

1. What does attachment research contribute to knowledge about child abuse victims?

2. If a woman is looking for a man who will share parenting responsibilites with her when the children come, how could she maximize the liklihood of getting what she is looking for?

ANSWERS WITH PAGE REFERENCES

Fill in the Blanks

1. mothers (181)
2. is not (182)
   5th to 6th (182)
   smiling (182)
3. decreases (183)
   exaggerated (183)
   extend (183)
4. withdrawal (183)
   delighted (187)
   crying (187)
5. less (187)
   learned helplessness
     (187)
   least (187)
6. insecurely (207)
   avoidant (207)
   aggressive (206)
   impulsiveness (206)
   cooperative (206)
7. temperament (190)
   easy (191)
   difficult (191)
   slow-to-warm-up (191)
8. "goodness of fit" (191)
9. noncuddler (190)
   noncuddlers (190)
   inborn (190)
10. physical (192)
    less (192)
    within (192)

11. playing with (193)
12. alone (196)
    independent (196)
    self-reliant (196)
13. attachment (197)
    separation anxiety (198)
14. sensitive period (204)
    eight (204)
    maturation (204)
    adaptive (204)
    mobility (204)
15. interact (200)
    security (205)
    relationship (206)
    insecurely (207)
16. four years (200)
    parents (201)
17. ethology (202)
18. autonomy (211)
    second (211)
    ability (211)
    stubborn and contrary
      (211)
    terrible twos (211)
    toilet (211)
19. socialization (211)
    parents (211)
20. timing (early or late)
      (212)
    manner (gentle or harsh)
      (212)

Multiple Choice

1. A (183)
2. B (187)
3. B (187)
4. B (190)
5. D (190)
6. A (192)
7. A (195-96)
8. B (197)
9. A (200)
10. C (203)
11. C (207)
12. D (199)
13. D (211)
14. B (212-13)
15. D (183)
16. A (184)
17. C (190)
18. D (191)
19. B (200)
20. C (212-13)
21. C (191)
22. D (203)
23. D (205)
24. C (211)
25. C (209)
26. A (204)
27. B (193)
28. A (187)
29. C (187)
30. B (199, 205)

SUGGESTED ANSWERS TO THOUGHT QUESTIONS

1. Children do form attachments, even to abusive parents. In fact, the pain of abuse may cause the child to cling even more intensely to the parent. Since attachment is likely to be present, the removal of a child from an abusive family may be traumatic for the child because of the disruption of the attachment. Any attempts at therapy for the child and abusive parents should also take into consideration the possibility that a sado-masochistic relationship may be present between the parents and the child--abuse leading to clinging, clinging leading to more abuse, etc.

2. She should look for a man who has demonstrated competence in child care. She should also look for someone with non-traditional employment so he can be at home more than someone who is traditionally employed. She should also be willing to work outside the home, at least partially, so the father will have time and opportunity to be the primary caregiver.

Chapter 7

The Beginnings of Intelligence and Language

AN OVERVIEW OF THE CHAPTER

Chapter Seven is about the beginnings of intelligence and language. The growth of intelligence, understanding, reasoning, and knowledge is called cognitive development. The major theory of cognitive development in childhood was put forward by Jean Piaget. Piaget's theory outlines four major periods of cognitive development. This chapter details Piaget's first major period, the sensorimotor period, which covers the first two years after birth. This sensorimotor period is subdivided into six stages. A number of cognitive milestones are reached in these two years: (1) learning what impact can be made on the world by one's actions, (2) the development of people and object permanence, which allows one to think about that which is not before one's eyes, (3) the ability to use language and (4) the development of self-awareness in which the child recognizes himself as an object in space. These changes result in the child becoming "able to keep track of more and more actions, objects, or ideas at the same time, and to combine them in increasingly complex ways."

After discussing the details of Piaget's sensorimotor period, your text presents research that has grown out of Piaget's theory. Increasingly inventive and sensitive research methods are being developed that experimentally test the phenomena that Piaget described. Such research is now suggesting that the beginnings of cognitive abilities are present even earlier than Piaget reported.

Early environment influences how much of the genetically determined cognitive potential can be reached. Research suggests that even some severe early deprivation can be overcome if the environment is enriched enough to compensate for it.

In addition to motor skill development, speech acquisition is one of the most obvious changes in early childhood. Even

70

though a child does not officially have language until he has 10
understandable words at about the age of 16 months, he has
already had much preparation for it. People (even children as
young as 4 years old) talk to babies in a special way that seems
to facilitate speech acquisition.

KEY TERMS AND CONCEPTS

cognitive development
adaptation
assimilation
accommodation
scheme
sensorimotor period
circular reaction
representations
deferred imitation
object permanence
sensorimotor play
mastery play

pretend play
symbolic play
stage 4 error
expressive jargon
receptive language
productive language
underextension
overextension
telegraphic speech
mean length of utterance (MLU)
motherese

CHAPTER OBJECTIVES--CHECK YOURSELF
By the time you've finished reading and studying this chapter,
you should be able to:

1. Explain examples of assimilation and accommodation in terms
    of adaptability.

2. Identify the six major stages of the sensorimotor period
    and describe the behaviors associated with each.

3. Describe the development of object permanence from stage 1
    through stage 6.

4. Describe the relationship between separation anxiety and
    person permanence.

5. Identify alternative explanations for stage 3 and stage 4
    infants' "object permanence" behavior.

6. Describe how the development of the self occurs.

7. Explain "stage-4 error."

8. Describe the impact cognitive advances have on social and
    emotional life.

9. Discuss rate of development as an indicator of
    intelligence.

10. Describe new research methodology that allows some prediction of future intelligence levels.

11. Discuss the impact of either enriched or deprived environments in infancy upon later intelligence.

12. Discuss the effects of malnutrition on intelligence.

13. Describe Lorber's research on people who have hydrocephalus and discuss the implications of that research for intellectual development.

14. Describe language development from birth to two years.

15. Explain what roles gender and birth order have on language acquisition.

16. Describe motherese and who uses it.

17. Describe the nonverbal signals that are part of conversational turn taking.

18. Summarize the results and implications of research attempts to teach language to chimps.

REVIEW EXERCISE--FILL IN THE BLANKS

1. _____ development is the growth of intelligence, understanding, reasoning, and knowledge.

2. According to Piaget, cognitive development depends on _____, or the gradual unfolding of a genetic plan, and on the child's _____ with the environment.

3. Piaget calls the first major period of development (roughly the first _____ years) the _____ period. It is subdivided into _____ stages. The units of cognition that Piaget uses are _____. These are first based on behaviors but later come to include mental events. New information is taken into these in a process called _____. If the basic unit of cognition must be adjusted to fit this new information, the process is known as _____.

4. Stage _____ involves the use and improvement of inborn schemes such as rooting, sucking and looking at things. Stage 2 marks the appearance of the first _____ adaptations, such as thumb-sucking. Piaget believes that schemes are acquired by means of _____ reactions which are the repetitions of behaviors that first happened at _____, but that the child then seeks to duplicate.

5. In Stage 3, the baby becomes interested in the effects he can produce on his _____. In stage 4, the baby demonstrates that he is able to more fully appreciate _____.

6. In Stage 5, babies begin to use active _____ to develop new schemes to suit new situations. In Stage 6, problems may be solved not only by trial and error, but also by a flash of _____. These children can think out possibilities and plan ahead by means of mental _____.

7. When a child does a(n) _____ imitation, she is using a _____ representation of something that happened previously.

8. In order to have mental representations, a baby must have mastered _____. The first hints of this appear in Stage _____.

9. Person permanence occurs a little _____ object permanence. Securely attached babies tend to develop "person permanence" and "object permanence" _____ than do insecurely attached babies.

10. The tendency of a Stage 4 baby to keep looking for something in a place that he found it previously has been labeled as the _____. It is more likely to occur if a _____ has occurred since the object was hidden.

11. Piaget and Freud agree that the newborn baby has no concept of _____ and cannot distinguish between _____ and _____. Around the middle of the second year, the baby begins to show signs of _____, silliness, or coyness when he sees his mirror image. By about age _____, the toddler can also identify pictures of himself.

12. _____ believes that the development of the child's self-image progresses hand-in-hand with his development of the concepts of object and person permanence.

13. Rate of development in the first year of life cannot be used to predict later _____; however, the baby's rate of _____ to stimuli is an important clue for later intelligence.

14. New data has indicated that low IQ's found in undernourished children were not due to starvation alone, but to malnutrition plus an unfavorable _____.

15. The brain is apparently able to adjust to a loss of size and of brain cells, provided that this loss occurs _____ in development. This refers to the _____ of brain. Studies of children with drastically reduced brain size due to _____ indicate that some of them function normally and some even exceptionally.

16. Most babies can say a word or two at _____ months of age. True speech is said to begin when the child uses _____ understandable words, usually about age _____. Some babies use _____, which sounds like speech but is unintelligible.

17. The baby's ability to understand the speech of the older people around her is called _____ language. At every age, it is greater than _____ language, the ability to express oneself in speech.

18. Language production starts to increase dramatically around _____ months. According to one theory, this increase comes at the point when the child has the insight that words are _____.

19. When children in the one-word stage use a word in a narrower way than an adult would, we call it an _____. When children in the one-word stage use a word in a broader way than an adult would, we call it _____. _____ speech consists only of key words, with endings and unimportant words left out.

20. One of the ways that psycholinguists measure the development of children's speech is with an index based on the length of utterances. It is called _____.

21. _____ is the name for the special language that older children and adults speak to very young children. Part of the purpose of this special speech seems to be for the infant to learn _____ interaction patterns.

22. Chimpanzees have been taught to communicate in _____ language. One chimp learned to make _____. Apparently the chimpanzees are unable to pick up on _____, which young children can do. The chimps do not engage in "word" usage just for the fun of it as young children do. It is suggested that chimpanzees use language as very young children who have not become aware that language _____ objects.

PRACTICE EXAM

1. Which of the following is an example of accommodation in the Piagetian sense?
   A. a focusing of the eyes
   B. fitting some new information into an existing form
   C. treating all dogs the same way
   D. modifying the notion that all dogs are friendly

74

2.   Circular reaction will begin to occur _____.
     A.   when the infant learns to crawl
     B.   during babbling
     C.   in stage 2
     D.   in stage 5

3.   In _____, a child first may perform a series of experiments
     just to see what will happen.
     A.   stage 5
     B.   stage 6
     C.   object permanence
     D.   separation anxiety

4.   Separation anxiety first occurs _____.
     A.   in stage 1
     B.   in stage 2
     C.   with the realization that mother is a permanent
          object
     D.   after object permanence

5.   In _____, a baby is likely to search for a hidden object
     in the place that he previously found it, even if he has
     since seen the object being hidden somewhere else.
     A.   stage 6   C.   stage 5
     B.   stage 3   D.   stage 4

6.   The concept of self _____.
     A.   is evidenced in babies shortly after birth
     B.   develops out of deferred imitation
     C.   does not develop until the baby can see herself in a
          mirror
     D.   develops gradually during infancy

7.   Present research suggests that _____.
     A.   severely undernourished children are permanently
          handicapped
     B.   children undernourished before birth are permanently
          handicapped
     C.   a good environment may counter some of the effects of
          early malnutrition on intelligence
     D.   an enriched environment can cause neurons to divide
          and multiply during the first two years of life

8.   True speech begins at about _____, when babies can produce
     ten understandable words.
     A.   one month after expressive jargon
     B.   9 months old
     C.   stage 3
     D.   15 months old

9. One intriguing explanation for the rapid rise in vocabulary of babies learning to talk involves _____.
   A. insight
   B. expressive jargon
   C. receptive language
   D. the emergence into stage 4

10. Which of the following is not characteristic of a mother's speech to her child?
   A. short sentences
   B. absence of questions
   C. many repetitions
   D. pauses between sentences

11. Psychologists who have used the MLU index have found _____.
   A. the "average" little girl progresses more rapidly than the "average" little boy
   B. there is a correlation between how early boys begin to speak and later intelligence
   C. environment plays little part in language development
   D. the MLU index is universal

12. Chimps are capable of all of the following **except** _____.
   A. naming things
   B. figuring out the rules of grammar
   C. using words
   D. combining two words

13. The first acquired adaptations are likely to occur during _____.
   A. stage 2
   B. language acquisition
   C. object permanence development
   D. stage 4

14. Babies become interested in the effect they can produce on the environment _____.
   A. in stage 5   C. in stage 6
   B. in stage 1   D. in stage 3

15. According to Piaget, play involves _____.
   A. exploration, experimentation, and practice
   B. symbiosis, symbolysis, and premeditation
   C. sensation, cognition, and emotion
   D. experimentation, imitation, and application

16. In _____, babies can use mental representations to think out the possibilities for solutions to problems.
   A. stage 4   C. stage 3
   B. stage 6   D. separation anxiety

17. There are differing views on when object permanence
    appears: Piaget says it appears in stage _____;
    Baillargeon concludes from his research that object
    permanence starts _____.
    A. 2; earlier
    B. 2; later
    C. 4; earlier
    D. 4; later

18. Children begin to recognize photos of themselves _____.
    A. in stage 5
    B. shortly after walking
    C. about the time of their first word
    D. around 21 months of age

19. Lorber's work on hydrocephalus shows _____.
    A. hydrocephaly to be correlated with early malnutrition
    B. that those with hydrocephaly rarely show normal
        intelligence
    C. that a brain reduced in size may not show any adverse
        effects if the reduction occurs before birth or early
        in infancy
    D. that there is little plasticity in the brain after
        birth

20. Which statement below best characterizes the relationship
    between receptive language and productive language?
    A. Productive language is greater than receptive language
        at an age of 9-12 months.
    B. Productive language tends to be greater than receptive
        language for children in one-parent homes.
    C. Receptive language is greater than productive language
        at every age.
    D. Productive language should be reinforced while
        receptive language is in extinction.

21. The use of telegraphic speech _____.
    A. begins to occur when children put words together at
        20 months
    B. won't emerge until children have a vocabulary of at
        least 150 words
    C. is an example of expressive jargon
    D. is the best example of receptive language

22. A child who says "feets," "goed," and "mines" probably
    _____.
    A. has no sense of the correct rules
    B. has discovered the general rules but is having
        problems with the exceptions
    C. has a mother who asks a lot of questions and stresses
        correct grammar
    D. is a noun user

23. A child who is calling a lamp, a flashlight, the sun and the moon all "hot" is _____.
    A. making a stage 4 error
    B. using an overextension
    C. displaying MLUs
    D. using expressive jargon

24. According to Piaget, a child who uses deferred imitation _____.
    A. has developed mental representation
    B. is discovering circular reaction patterns
    C. is practicing telegraphic speech
    D. is avoiding people permanence

25. The most complex emotion in the following list is _____.
    A. pleasure   C. fear
    B. distress   D. jealousy

26. The habituation test indicates _____.
    A. intelligence
    B. language utilization level
    C. stage-4 errors
    D. object permanence

27. An early example of emotions affecting learning is: _____.
    A. children high in the distress index habituate more quickly
    B. the prolonged use of expressive jargon
    C. person permanence comes earlier in "securely attached" children
    D. "difficult" babies are slow to develop object permanence

28. If your neighbor proudly describes her 10-month-old son as having started to pretend to drive a car when he is in his high chair, _____.
    A. she is probably correct
    B. she is probably incorrect
    C. she is making a stage-4 error
    D. the baby is making a stage-4 error

29. In a mother-child interaction, the most beneficial language learning results when _____.
    A. mother decides what they will look at
    B. baby decides what they will look at
    C. mother and baby take turns deciding what to look at
    D. attention is free-floating and undirected

30. "Smart" babies may cause their mothers to intellectually stimulate them which facilitates further cognitive development. This is an example of _____.
   A. transactive interaction of heredity and environment
   B. overextension and underextension
   C. critical period acceleration
   D. "Barbadian neurological milestones"

THOUGHT QUESTIONS

1. How might knowing the information in this chapter affect the care you would give to 6-month-old?

2. How would the chapter information affect care given to an 18-month-old?

3. Since the mother's responsiveness toward her baby affects his cognitive development. how could the mother's responsiveness be improved?

4. What effect on language acquisition might be seen in the child from a bilingual home?

ANSWERS WITH PAGE REFERENCES

Fill in the Blanks

1. cognitive (218)
2. maturation (218)
   interactions (218)
3. two (221)
   sensorimotor (221)
   six (221)
   schemes (218)
   assimilation (218)
   accommodation (218)
4. one (219)
   acquired (219)
   circular (219)
   random (219)
5. environment (219)
   cause and effect (220)
6. experimentation (220)
   insight (221)
   representation (222)
7. deferred (222)
   mental (222)
8. object permanence (222)
   three (223)
9. before (224)
   earlier (224)

10. Stage 4 error (231)
    time delay (231)
11. self (228)
    "me" (228)
    "not me" (228)
    self consciousness (229)
    21 months (229)
12. Piaget (229)
13. I.Q. (234)
    habituation (234)
14. environment (241)
15. early (241)
    plasticity (341)
    hydrocephaly (241)
16. 12 (242)
    ten (243)
    16 months (243)
    expressive jargon (243)
17. receptive (243)
    productive (244)
18. eighteen (244)
    representations (244)
19. underextension (245)
    overextension (245)
    telegraphic (246)

20. mean length of
    utterance (247)
21. motherese (249)
    conversational (250)

22. sign (253)
    130 signs (253)
    grammar (254)
    represents (254)

Multiple Choice

1.	D (218)	9.	A (244)	17.	C (230)	25.	D (233)
2.	C (219)	10.	B (248)	18.	D (229)	26.	A (234)
3.	B (220)	11.	A (248)	19.	C (241)	27.	C (224)
4.	C (224)	12.	B (254)	20.	C (243)	28.	B (227)
5.	D (225)	13.	A (219)	21.	A (246)	29.	B (248)
6.	D (228)	14.	D (219)	22.	B (254)	30.	A (238)
7.	C (241)	15.	A (226)	23.	B (245)		
8.	D (243)	16.	B (222)	24.	A (228)		

SUGGESTED ANSWERS TO THOUGHT QUESTIONS

1. For the six-month-old (Piaget's stage 3) I would increase
the effect he can have on his environment. Beside
letting him elicit predictable response from me, I would
place him (on his back or propped in an infant seat
arrangement) where his hands or feet would occasionally
hit hanging objects so that he could engage in circular
reaction patterns with the objects if he wanted to do so.
    Since caregiver response to baby is so important, I
would increase the number and duration of periods where
baby and I are interacting together on a point of interest
that baby has chosen. I would carry him on expeditions
around his familiar surroundings to show him things up
close that he normally sees at a distance, and name them
for him. I would be particularly sensitive to which
stimuli seem to be the most interesting to him, and allow
him frequent opportunities to enjoy them.
    I would engage in conversational games of babbling.
If this child is not the only child in the situation, I
would want to realize he is probably not getting as much
verbal stimulation as he would if he were an only child. I
would try to make sure I talked to him at every appropriate
opportunity.

2. For the 18-month-old (Piaget stage 5-6) I would provide a
variety of toys and media (water, sand, and play dough)
with which she could actively experiment.
    I would initiate some play-pretend activities with an
object used for some unusual pretend purpose or with
imaginary objects according to the child's level.
    For self awareness I would engage in some games based
on looking in a full-length mirror. There would be a
picture gallery including the child and others in the
environment placed at child-eye level. He and I could

engage in a name-the-person-in-the-picture game.

   This chapter would also make me aware that an 18-month old's emotions are becoming more complex, and that the beginnings of jealousy may be possible. I would want to be sensitive to possible jealousy situations.

3.   First, let the mother know how important her responsiveness is so her motivation might be increased. Another factor may be the amount of time that the mother has to spend with the child. Her responsiveness might be improved if she had more relaxed time with him; therefore, teaching her to do better at time management might help.
   The mother might also benefit from some training to increase her sensitivity to her baby. Aside from taking a course in child psychology to learn more about her baby, she could be shown a videotape of samples of interactions of mothers and babies which point out how each mother is responding to the cues from her baby. More intensive intervention would be to have a panel of trained people watch a videotape of the woman and her baby and help her to see the cues that her baby gives, but to which she does not respond.

4.   Perhaps a child from a bilingual family would tend to gain quicker insight into the arbitrary assignment of sounds to name objects, since he experiences two different names for the same objects in his home. His rate of grammar acquisition may be slowed or enhanced by having different grammars to learn, particularly in the case of languages with radically different grammars.

Chapter 8

The Preschool Child

AN OVERVIEW OF THE CHAPTER

In Chapter Eight the text discusses the physical, motor, and perceptual development of the preschool child. By the age of 2 1/2, the toddler has become a "preschooler." The preschooler is noticeably more advanced than the toddler in appearance, in behavior, and in the ability to communicate. The 2 1/2-year old boy is more than 50% of his adult height but only about 20% of his adult weight. Growth during the preschool period is considerably slower than growth during the first 2 1/2 years.

Physical maturation enables the preschooler to engage in vigorous, sustained activity. There are improvements in both large-muscle (whole body) and small muscle (fine manipulation) skills. While many of these developmental changes are the result of maturation, environmental effects such as nutrition play an important role in determining whether these built-in processes proceed normally. There are some variations in the development of motor skills between boys and girls. As a result of these changes, the preschooler is better able than the toddler to participate in the society to which he belongs. This participation ultimately contributes to his social and cognitive development.

By the age of 2 1/2 years, a child's brain is 75% complete. Although brain growth has slowed by the age of 2, the neurons continue to increase in size. Also, the process of myelination is still going on. The two hemispheres of the brain serve different functions. The left side of the brain, which controls the right side of the body, is generally used for language, reasoning, and numerical skills. The right side, which controls the left side of the body, specializes in nonverbal skills such as spatial ability, perception of patterns and melodies, and the expression and recognition of emotions.

Infants show no strong tendency to use one hand or the

other. By the preschool period, however, most children favor
the right hand. The tendency to be right-handed appears to be a
built-in characteristic of the human species. Left- and right-
handed children do not differ significantly in intelligence or
in motor skills. Left-handers, however, do show up more
frequently than would be expected among groups of "exceptional"
children--those with learning disabilities, autism or
retardation, as well as those who are especially gifted or
creative. The way left-handers use the various parts of their
brains may confer either an advantage or a handicap, depending
on the circumstances.

Basic perceptual abilities--the ability to see, hear and
integrate sensory information--are well established by the
preschool period. Perceptual constancies, the ability to
perceive things as they "really are," seem to be largely built-
in, and show themselves at an early age. Practicing these
innate abilities improves the preschooler's performance on
perceptual tasks, however, again emphasizing the importance of a
stimulating environment. The chapter also summarizes research
on perceptual constancies and on how children look at pictures.
Special sections deal with the effects of AIDS on children and
the artistry of the preschool child.

KEY TERMS AND CONCEPTS

preschool period	small-muscle skills
preschooler	lateralization
acquired immune deficiency	projective size
syndrome (AIDS)	size constancy
HIV virus	shape constancy
bilateral coordination	fixate
large-muscle skills	tadpole person

CHAPTER OBJECTIVES--CHECK YOURSELF
By the time you've finished reading and studying this chapter,
you should be able to:

1. Describe the physical changes that make the preschooler's
    body different from the infant's body.

2. Discuss the importance of good nutrition for intellectual
    and physical development.

3. Discuss the practical suggestions offered in the text for
    ensuring that the preschooler's diet is an adequate one.

4. List the major health issues for preschoolers as discussed
    in your text. Include a reference to acquired immune
    deficiency syndrome (AIDS).

5. List the changes that occur in motor development during the preschool years. Make references to large-muscle and small-muscle skills, body perception and bilateral coordination.

6. Enumerate the sex differences in motor development during the preschool years.

7. Discuss the unique functions of the left and right hemispheres of the brain.

8. Explain the current theory of handedness and show how this relates to brain lateralization.

9. Compare and contrast the behavioral and psychological characteristics of right-handers and left-handers.

10. Summarize the studies that were done to investigate and help reduce children's left-right confusions.

11. Explain what perceptual constancies are and how they are acquired. Give examples of size and shape constancies.

12. Summarize studies dealing with a child's ability to interpret pictures.

13. Describe the differences in eye movements of adults and young children as they look at pictures, and state the implications for the way children see the world.

14. Describe the "tadpole person" typically drawn by preschoolers, and explain what such drawings suggest about children's motor skills and their perceptions of people.

HELPFUL HINT

Book publishers and students do not always see eye to eye on "boxes" with special information inserted into a text. The writer or publisher puts the information in the box to attract the attention of the reader--it is a special section that the student might find interesting. Students, on the other hand, often conclude that since the information is put in a box, it is not part of the "real" text and therefore can be ignored. Professors tend to side with the book publishers on this issue, though, and very often test questions are based on boxed material. You might ask your instructor how boxed material will be treated.

REVIEW EXERCISE--FILL IN THE BLANKS

1. At 2 /12 years of age, toddlerhood is over and the _____ period has begun.

2. A 2 1/2 year-old boy has achieved more than _____ percent of his adult height, but only about _____ percent of his adult weight. His brain growth is more than _____ percent complete.

3. Preschool boys are physically _____ than preschool girls. In other areas, such as coordination and growth of permanent teeth, preschool girls are _____ advanced than the boys.

4. Preschoolers eat _____ (more/less) food than toddlers, and they tend to be very _____ eaters. With regard to nutrition, the most common dietary deficiency is for _____.

5. Bribing a child to eat foods he doesn't like is a _____ idea. Restricting fats in a child's diet is a _____ idea.

6. The greatest threat to a child's life in our society today is _____.

7. A fatal disease caused by the HIV virus and often transmitted from infected mothers to their children either before or during birth is _____.

8. Another health hazard to children often associated with flaking paint in old buildings is _____.

9. Whole-body kinds of activities are also called _____ skills. Activities requiring the coordination of muscles for the fine manipulation of objects are called _____ skills.

10. Three factors involved in the development of motor skills are the establishment of _____ muscle control, an increasingly accurate perception of one's _____, and the development of _____ coordination.

11. The process of seeing what you are doing and then changing what you are doing so you come closer to your goal is known as eye-hand _____.

12. Some differences in motor development among preschoolers are _____, or inherited, but boys or girls may also be better at some activities because by doing them a lot they get more _____.

13. While preschoolers have almost all the brain cells they are going to have, neurons continue to get _____ and the process of _____ of axons continues for some time to come.

14. The two sides of the brain look the same but they serve different functions. First, each side controls movements in the _____ side of the body. Also the _____ side is more devoted to language skills while the _____ side is more involved with spatial abilities and other non-verbal activities. _____ abilities use both sides of the brain.

15. When brain damage occurs, the younger you are, the _____ likely you are to recover. This is an example of the _____ of young brains.

16. The tendency of the two halves of the brain to serve different functions is called _____.

17. A preference for the use of one hand or the other develops by the time a child is a _____. Most people end up being _____ handed. This seems to be a _____ characteristic of human beings.

18. The brains of left-handed people seem to be _____ (more/less) lateralized than the brains of right-handers. More retarded or learning disabled children, as well as children who are gifted in music and math seem to be _____ handed than one would expect by chance alone.

19. Tests of manual dexterity are best performed by children who _____ (have/have not) established a dominant hand. One reason for this might be that children with a dominant hand give that hand more _____ in manual skills.

20. Telling left from right in preschoolers is easier if the task is related to the _____ instead of being symbolic. Once a child has chosen a dominant hand, it is _____ to teach the child left from right.

21. The _____ size and shape of an object is related to the image it produces in the eye from a given perspective.

22. Perceptual processes that allow us to see things the way they "really are" are called _____. Two examples are _____ and _____. While the processes themselves appear to be _____, they do improve with practice.

23. The ability to recognize objects in pictures seems to be _____ (innate/learned). But children do not look at pictures in the same way as adults. Adults scan a picture _____, and the ability to study a picture for its content seems to be a _____ skill instead of a perceptual one.

24. Children's early drawings of people, a head with legs attached, are called _____ people. Children who produce such drawings generally _____ (do/do not) know how people really look.

PRACTICE EXAM

1. At the age of two and a half years, a child _____.
    A.   is about half his adult height
    B.   is about half his adult weight
    C.   has a disproportionately small head
    D.   has disproportionately long legs

2. In comparison to boys, preschool girls _____.
    A.   are slightly taller
    B.   are slightly heavier
    C.   lose their baby teeth earlier
    D.   have less fat on their bodies

3. The most prevalent deficiency in the diet of American
    children seems to be that of _____.
    A.   iron
    B.   vitamin A
    C.   vitamin C
    D.   refined sugar

4. As preschoolers progress into school age, their bodies
    assume more adult proportions. This means _____.
    A.   the skull gets smaller
    B.   internal organs grow faster than the rest of the body
    C.   the neck gets shorter
    D.   the arms and legs grow faster than the head or trunk

5. Compared with the toddler, the preschooler _____.
    A.   eats a larger variety of foods
    B.   doesn't need as much sleep
    C.   is less active
    D.   breathes faster

6. The preschooler's advances in motor control partially
    depend on _____.
    A.   habituation
    B.   adaptation
    C.   maturation
    D.   extrapolation

7. Compared to preschool girls, preschool boys _____.
    A.   have less muscle
    B.   have more fat
    C.   are taller and heavier
    D.   are better at fine manipulation skills

8. A study of preschoolers in a nursery school showed that boys spent much more of their time in vigorous outdoor play, while the girls spent relatively more time indoors. The investigators concluded that this was due in part to _____.
   A. the behavior of the nursery school staff
   B. the child rearing practices of the parents
   C. biological differences
   D. the nature of the available apparatus

9. The most common threat to a preschooler's health comes from _____.
   A. accidents
   B. AIDS
   C. malnutrition
   D. contagious diseases

10. In most cases, the left hemisphere of the brain is in charge of _____.
    A. the right side of the body
    B. the left side of the body
    C. spatial abilities
    D. the expression of emotions

11. Fifteen year old Lou Ann was in an accident that caused damage to the language area of her brain. Her chances of recovery and regaining normal language abilities are _____.
    A. better than those of preschooler
    B. about the same as those of a toddler
    C. worse than those of a preschooler
    D. better than those of an infant

12. Right-handedness _____.
    A. is just our particular society's tradition
    B. seems to be the result of inherited characteristics
    C. is best for all children
    D. is a recessive trait

13. Perceptual constancies are _____.
    A. symptoms of a learning disability
    B. learned as we discover what size and shape objects "really are"
    C. apparently automatic and innate
    D. usually outgrown by the age of five

14. Little Waldo has always been ambidextrous. This means he will tend to eat or throw a ball _____.
    A. with his left hand only
    B. with his right hand only
    C. with either hand
    D. with both hands at once

15. When little Waldo grows up and his wife shouts, "Quick!
    Turn left here!" while he is driving a car, he is likely to
    _____.
    A.   turn left automatically
    B.   turn left or right unpredictably
    C.   turn right every time
    D.   none of the above: ambidextrous people cannot drive

16. The best way to teach a young child left from right is to
    _____.
    A.   use mirror-image symbols such as the letters "b" and
         "d"
    B.   use concrete "real-world" examples such as objects on
         a table
    C.   use mental imagery
    D.   do it before he is three years old

17. Growth during the preschool period is _____ than growth
    during infancy.
    A.   considerably slower
    B.   considerably faster
    C.   about the same
    D.   more unpredictable

18. Which of the following is not one of the factors important
    in the development of motor skills?
    A.   bilateral coordination
    B.   egocentrism
    C.   accurate body image
    D.   voluntary movement

19. Preschoolers tend to eat _____.
    A.   only foods with which they are familiar
    B.   more than they ought to unless the parents watch them
         carefully
    C.   almost anything that is put on their plate
    D.   in binge patterns

20. Today's highly processed foods seem to _____.
    A.   have caused an increase in the rate of retardation
    B.   have adverse affects on the learning process
    C.   increase the likelihood of antisocial behavior
    D.   have no detrimental effect on children's growth or
         health

21. Most children with AIDS _____.
    A.   acquired it prenatally or during birth
    B.   contracted the disease from being around infected
         brothers or sisters
    C.   will grow up to produce AIDS babies of their own
    D.   are recipients of tainted blood transfusions

22. The coordination of the two halves of the body is called
_____.
   A. bilateral coordination
   B. bifocal coordination
   C. lateralization
   D. bilateralization

23. Which of the following may be inherited in connection with
motor development?
   A. physique
   B. a talent for coordinated movements
   C. a tendency to be more active than other children
   D. all of the above

24. If a child is diagnosed as having AIDS, the best approach
is to provide appropriate medical care and to _____.
   A. keep him or her away from other children to prevent
       contagion
   B. treat the child as normally as possible
   C. avoid touching the child's skin
   D. test the mother for AIDS as well, since she may have
       gotten it from the child during pregnancy

25. For most people, the right hemisphere of the brain controls
_____.
   A. the right side of the body
   B. language
   C. nonverbal skills
   D. numerical skills

26. Studies of lateralization have shown that _____.
   A. brain activity is greatest in the right hemisphere
       when the baby is hearing speech
   B. the two hemispheres start off equal
   C. the two hemispheres aren't the same, even in very
       young babies
   D. the young human brain is very inflexible

27. Left-handed children _____.
   A. are more intelligent than right-handed children
   B. are better at using their non-dominant hand than are
       right-handed children
   C. should be switched to right-handedness for convenience
   D. have poorly organized brains

28. You might expect that 4-year old children who did worse on
a test of manual dexterity which involved putting beads
on a string or putting beans in a bottle were _____.
   A. right-handed
   B. left-handed
   C. especially creative
   D. the ones who hadn't established a dominant hand

29. When looking at pictures, children tend to _____.
    A. ignore the edges
    B. use longer eye movements
    C. scan systematically
    D. sweep around the picture as a whole

30. The type of person that a 3 1/2- or 4-year old draws which has no body--only a big head with some sticks for legs--is called a _____.
    A. stick man
    B. skeleton person
    C. funny man
    D. tadpole person

THOUGHT QUESTIONS

1. Imagine that you are a psychologist discussing motor development with the parents of twins, Linda and Larry, aged three. What would you tell the parents when they say they are concerned that their children are so different from one another?

2. You begin to suspect that your child is showing tendencies toward left-handedness. What does this mean? What should you do about it?

3. If you were going to draw illustrations for a children's book, how would the information in this chapter influence your style of illustration?

ANSWERS WITH PAGE REFERENCES

Fill in the Blanks

1. preschool (258)
2. fifty (259)
   twenty (259)
   seventy-five (259)
3. taller and heavier (260)
   more (260)
4. less (261)
   picky (261)
   iron (262)
5. bad (261)
   bad (262)
6. accidents (263)
7. AIDS (264)
8. lead poisoning (263)
9. large-muscle (268)
   small-muscle (269)

10. voluntary (267)
    body (267)
    bilateral (268)
11. coordination (269)
12. genetic (271)
    practice (272)
13. bigger (273)
    myelination (273)
14. opposite (273)
    left (273)
    right (273)
    Cognitive (274)
15. more (274)
    plasticity (274)
16. lateralization (274)

17. preschooler (275)
    right (275)
    innate (275)
18. less (275)
    left (275)
19. have (276)
    practice (276)
20. real world (277)
    easier (278)

21. projective (279)
22. constancies (279)
    size constancy (280)
    shape constancy (280)
    innate (280)
23. innate (281)
    systematically (282)
    cognitive (282)
24. tadpole (283)
    do (284)

Multiple Choice

1.	A (259)	9.	A (263)	17.	A (260)	25.	C (273)
2.	C (260)	10.	A (273)	18.	B (267)	26.	C (274)
3.	A (262)	11.	C (274)	19.	A (261)	27.	B (275)
4.	D (260)	12.	B (275)	20.	D (262)	28.	D (276)
5.	B (265)	13.	C (280)	21.	A (264)	29.	A (282)
6.	C (266)	14.	C (278)	22.	A (268)	30.	D (283)
7.	C (260)	15.	B (278)	23.	D (271)		
8.	C (272)	16.	B (277)	24.	B (265)		

SUGGESTED ANSWERS TO THOUGHT QUESTIONS

1. First, there is a wide variation in the rate at which children develop motor skills. Since Larry and Linda are fraternal twins, that means they are no more alike genetically than ordinary brothers and sisters. Since they are different sexes, you would expect all the common differences between boys and girls to be present. List these differences again.

2. Left-handed tendencies mean that the child is settling into a brain lateralization pattern in which each side shares more of the control of different functions than is common in right-handers. While there are statistically more left-handers in groups of children with certain kinds of problems, there is also the possibility that the child might be above average in certain skills or abilities. The most likely outcome is that the child will be perfectly normal. It is not advisable to force the child to change to being right-handed. That may cause stress and problems of its own.

3. Since preschoolers tend to look at limited portions of a picture and also tend to overlook subtle details, one might keep in mind that elaborate illustrations with rich detail will probably impress the adults who view the book more than the children for whom it is intended. The children will come to appreciate the detail more as they grow older. In the meanwhile, if the pictures are intended to convey important information about the story, keep them simple and to the point.

Chapter 9

Preschoolers Think
and Communicate

AN OVERVIEW OF THE CHAPTER

Chapter Nine investigates how preschoolers think and communicate. There are three main areas of focus: the characteristics of preoperational thought, intelligence, and language development.

Piaget believed that thought in this period is "qualitatively different" from thought in older children and adults. He calls preschoolers' thoughts "egocentric," by which he means that they can see a situation only from their own point of view. Other, more recent research, has found that a preschooler can imagine what someone else's viewpoint is like if that viewpoint is simpler and more "real-world" oriented than the one the child sees herself. Also, according to Piaget, preschoolers are unable to "decenter"—they cannot consider more than one aspect of a situation at once. Again, more recent evidence shows that while preschoolers do seem to be very easily swayed by appearances, they are still likely to respond correctly in the absence of misleading sensory evidence. In sum, while the evidence for a "qualitative difference" between preschool thought and the thinking of older children is not as impressive as Piaget believed, there is certainly a quantitative difference. Cognitive development from the preschool years on is more gradual and continuous. Representational thought, especially symbolic thought, makes preschoolers' mental abilities a clear step above those of infants and toddlers.

IQ tests given to preschoolers correlate reasonably well with IQ scores obtained in later childhood and adulthood. Performance on IQ tests is not, however, always a good measure of intelligence. "Intelligence" refers to qualities such as the ability to learn quickly, to reason correctly with words and numbers, to understand spoken or written words and sentences, to see relationships and differences between things, to think up

insightful solutions to problems, and the like. Children from
different cultural backgrounds, family circumstances and
socioeconomic levels may not always demonstrate these abilities
equally on a standardized test. The differences may not stem
from variations in innate ability, but rather from differences
in what their environments have taught them.

The most impressive achievement in the preschool period is
in the realm of language development. The average 2-year old
has a vocabulary of only 200 or 300 words and speaks mostly in
2- or 3-word sentences. In contrast, 6-year olds have a
productive vocabulary of around 2500 words and a receptive
vocabulary of up to 14,000 words. They speak in complex
sentences and demonstrate a sophisticated grasp of the grammar
of their language.

Language develops in virtually every child, under an
incredibly wide range of environmental conditions. This is true
for all but the most severely retarded or brain-damaged
children. The environment does have an effect on what kind of
language a child will learn and on how well he will learn it.
There is a relationship between how well children speak and
various measures of the parent's speech to the child. Children
who spend a lot of time talking with adult caregivers are more
verbally advanced.

The chapter includes a special section on "metacognition"
(which is learning how to learn) and on "private speech" (which
is when young children talk to themselves). A final section
deals with the question of whether or not preschool enrichment
programs boost IQ.

KEY TERMS AND CONCEPTS

preoperational period	validity
decenter	mental age
egocentric	intelligence quotient
center	Stanford-Binet
intellectual realism	WISC-R
phenomenism	WPPSI
one-to-one correspondence	error of measurement
rule	reliability
cardinality rule	fast mapping
order-irrelevance principle	class inclusion problem
cardinality principle	grammatical morphemes
metacognition	tag question
rehearsal	private speech
categorization	

CHAPTER OBJECTIVES--CHECK YOURSELF

By the time you've finished reading and studying this chapter, you should be able to:

1. Describe the characteristics of preoperational thinking in Piagetian terms.

2. Discuss the evidence and/or arguments against egocentrism in the preschooler.

3. Describe how well a preschooler is able to distinguish between reality and fantasy. Include a distinction between fantasy and pretense.

4. Describe conservation of volume and conservation of number, and explain why Piaget's work on these topics is now seen as incomplete.

5. List and describe the three processes involved in counting.

6. Define metacognition and compare preschoolers with older children on this ability.

7. Describe what intelligence tests measure and how modern intelligence tests were developed.

8. Explain how the intelligence quotient is calculated and why this formula is no longer used.

9. Identify likely causes for variation in IQ scores for the same children tested at different times.

10. Define the terms validity and reliability as applied to IQ tests.

11. Summarize and evaluate the various efforts to improve IQs for disadvantaged preschoolers.

12. Summarize the differences between the way adults speak to each other and the way they speak to children, and explain how this affects children's language development.

13. Define grammatical morphemes and describe their sequence of appearance in children's language.

14. Explain why the sequence of appearance of grammatical morphemes in children occurs as it does.

15. Describe the development and use of negatives and questions in children's language.

16. Summarize the research done on the effects of environment on language acquisition.

17. Compare and contrast Piaget's and Vygotsky's interpretation of the purpose of "private speech."

REVIEW EXERCISE--FILL IN THE BLANKS

1. According to Piaget, preschoolers are in the _____ period. His word for expressing the quality of their thought process is _____, which means they judge everything from their own point of view.

2. Other researchers have shown that preschoolers can imagine someone else's point of view, but only when that viewpoint reflects _____ (objective/projective) reality. They _____ (do/do not) like scenes where objects overlap each other.

3. According to _____, the child comes to understand another viewpoint in two steps, or levels.

4. The ability to consider more than one aspect of a situation at a time is what Piaget called the ability to _____. More recent research shows that while children may fail a test involving _____ of liquid volume, the reason may be simply the inability to tell _____ from _____.

5. If a child responds in terms of reality when asked to respond in terms of appearances, this is called _____. If a child responds in terms of appearances when asked to respond in terms of reality, this is _____.

6. _____, the ability to consciously imagine something other than reality, occurs early in childhood and appears to be universal.

7. Four- and five-year olds seem to understand conservation of number if the number of objects is no more than _____. The three principles that must be understood before one can successfully count a row of objects are: _____, _____ and _____.

8. The ability to understand, think about, and monitor the progress of one's own cognitive processes is _____.

9. IQ tests are designed to measure _____. A test that measures what it claims to be measuring is _____. Evidence that IQ tests have some _____ is the fact that they do pretty well in predicting how children will do in _____.

10. The first famous, successful IQ test was invented by _____. IQ stands for _____. It was obtained by dividing the child's _____ by his _____ and multiplying by _____.

11. The IQ formula fails to accurately represent intelligence when it is applied to the test results of _____.

12. Three intelligence tests commonly used on children today are the _____, the _____, and the _____.

13. If a test is _____, it will give approximately the same results when a child retakes it. If this doesn't happen, it may be that the child has changed in her cognitive abilities, or that the test has a large _____.

14. Preschool enrichment programs seem to produce the best results among children who are truly _____. Even then, however, the effects of the program may be _____.

15. The average two-year old knows about _____ words. By the time he is six, that number has risen to about _____ productive words.

16. _____ is a quick method for getting the approximate meaning of a new word.

17. Preschoolers have trouble with words that are multiple names for the same thing. This leads them to fail on Piaget's _____ problem.

18. When an adult speaks to a child, she typically uses general terms for a class of things only when the object being referred to is _____ of the class being discussed.

19. Prepositions such as "in" or "on," and suffixes such as "ing" and "ed" are called _____. Children acquire the proper use of these prepositions and suffixes in an order determined by the _____ of the rules governing their use.

20. The development of language appears to be an _____ characteristic among human beings. Only the most _____ or _____ children fail to learn language. The _____, of course, determines which language a child will speak.

21. The best way for a child to acquire language is to take an _____ role in interacting with someone speaking that language. The better the teacher, the better the learning that occurs. _____ children learn language faster and better than do later children, because the _____ spends most of his time speaking with the _____, while later children spend more time speaking with their _____.

22. Talking aloud to yourself is called _____. Recent research suggests that this process helps the child to _____ his own behavior.

PRACTICE EXAM

1. In Piagetian terms, preschoolers are in which period?
   A. sensorimotor
   B. preoperational
   C. operational
   D. concrete operations

2. Recent studies on "point of view" show that the preschooler generally chooses _____.
   A. his own view
   B. the other's point of view
   C. the "good" view
   D. a view in which one thing partially overlaps another

3. Piaget would say that _____.
   A. language makes thinking possible
   B. one doesn't develop language until one can think
   C. preschoolers' thought processes are qualitatively different from those of older children
   D. language and cognitive abilities are not related

4. According to Piaget, an example of not being able to decenter would be _____.
   A. private speech
   B. inability to conserve
   C. conservation of number
   D. tag questions

5. Jennifer, aged 3, plays hide and seek by hiding her face behind her hands. Does she really believe the seeker can't see her?
   A. Yes, if by "seeing her" you mean making eye contact
   B. No, she is just being silly
   C. Yes, she believes she becomes invisible when she is unable to see someone else
   D. No, she is simply trying to confuse the other child

6. Research indicates that preschool children _____.
   A. are entirely egocentric
   B. modify their speech to meet the needs of the speaker
   C. like views in which one object blocks another
   D. can do better at switching points of view than Piaget thought

7. The principle which says it doesn't matter in what order you count objects, the total will still be the same, is called _____.
   A. paired associates
   B. order dependence
   C. centering
   D. order irrelevance

8. Learning to learn and thinking about thinking are examples
   of _____.
   A.   intransigence
   B.   metacognition
   C.   inactive representations
   D.   egocentricity

9. Responding to what is really there when asked to respond in
   terms of appearances only is called _____.
   A.   perseveration
   B.   categorical blindness
   C.   intellectual realism
   D.   phenomenism

10. A child who says that the amount of liquid has changed when
    it is poured into a tall, skinny glass is _____.
    A.   being egotistical
    B.   responding in terms of phenomenism
    C.   demonstrating conservation of volume
    D.   unable to disregard reality

11. Preschoolers will probably do better at conservation of
    numbers than Piaget would predict as long as _____.
    A.   the number is small enough—four or less
    B.   the child is allowed to practice first
    C.   the objects to be counted are favorite toys
    D.   there are no distractions

12. The cardinality rule is: _____.
    A.   the last number you used is the total number
    B.   always count from left to right
    C.   one number for one object
    D.   even numbers come before odd numbers

13. The order-irrelevancy rule is: _____.
    A.   numbers can be used in any order
    B.   it makes no difference which order you count things in
    C.   spacing objects further apart does not change the
         number of them
    D.   larger objects do not weigh more than smaller objects

14. A test that measures what it is supposed to measure _____.
    A.   is valid
    B.   has reliability
    C.   will have no error of measurement
    D.   is the easiest kind of test to construct

15. Mental age _____.
    A.   is the child's actual age
    B.   multiplied by chronological age equals IQ
    C.   shows the child's level of intellectual skill
    D.   decreases with age

16. Which of the following is a pointless thing to say to a
    three-year old?
    A.   Think about what you are doing!
    B.   Repeat after me.
    C.   How many fingers is this? (holding up two)
    D.   Come to Mommy!

17. The American version of the Binet IQ test, developed by
    Lewis Terman, was called the _____.
    A.   Simon-Binet
    B.   Stanford-Binet
    C.   Carley-Simon
    D.   WISC

18. Which of the following statements about IQ test score
    stability is most correct?
    A.   IQ scores of children are totally unpredictable.
    B.   IQ scores of most children increase steadily with age.
    C.   For some children, variation in IQ is probably due
         to error of measurement.
    D.   Most school placements can safely be made on the basis
         of an IQ score obtained at the age of two.

19. A test which is not very much affected by chance factors
    or day-to-day variations is said to be _____.
    A.   valid
    B.   reliable
    C.   representative
    D.   functional

20. WPPSI stands for _____.
    A.   Wisconsin Preschool Placement Standards Inventory
    B.   World Piagetian Parent Studies Institute
    C.   Washington Parent Participation Seminars, Inc.
    D.   Weschler Preschool and Primary Scale of Intelligence

21. Operation Head Start _____.
    A.   generally produced long-term gains in IQ scores
    B.   was an enrichment program designed for disadvantaged
         preschoolers
    C.   yielded good short-term results, as well as improved
         performance throughout the primary grades
    D.   placed children from good backgrounds in school a
         year early

22. Roger Brown's work on the acquisition of grammatical
    morphemes _____.
    A.   found that grammatical morphemes appeared in a
         fairly predictable and orderly sequence
    B.   found that the order of appearance was based on the
         frequency of use
    C.   used nonsense words such as zib and wug
    D.   found a random order of appearance

23. By the time a child is in the late preschool years, she can probably understand about _____ words.
    A. 300
    B. 1000
    C. 2500
    D. 14,000

24. A rapid method of approximating the meaning of a new word by using context and mutual exclusion is _____.
    A. phenomenizing
    B. extrapolation
    C. interleaving
    D. fast mapping

25. The environment will most likely not affect _____.
    A. the kind of language a child acquires
    B. whether or not the child will acquire language at all
    C. how well the child speaks the language she learns
    D. the size of the child's vocabulary

26. Which of the following is not true of the preschooler's conversational skills?
    A. They know that they are supposed to talk when the interviewer stops talking.
    B. They know that when the interviewer asks a question, they are supposed to answer.
    C. They know what form the answer should take.
    D. They are able to judge whether the listener has understood them.

27. In a recent study of the effects of environment on language development in preschool children in Bermuda Bay day care centers, a very important factor proved to be _____.
    A. how long they stayed at the center
    B. how much time they spoke with younger children
    C. how much time they spoke with older children
    D. how much time they spoke with adult caregivers

28. Vygotsky believed that the private speech of preschoolers _____.
    A. was children's way of regulating their own behavior
    B. was yet another indication of egocentrism
    C. reflects their inability to think without talking
    D. gradually disappears because of social pressure

29. When parents name objects for children, when do they tend to ignore class names and use specific individual labels?
    A. when the class name is longer than seven letters
    B. when the class includes more than five different types
    C. when the object is not representative of the class
    D. when the child is female

30. Which of the following is representative of the earliest form of question-asking in children?
   A. Please mother, when do you expect father to return from the office?
   B. Is Dad home yet?
   C. Daddy home?
   D. Daddy not home, is he?

THOUGHT QUESTIONS

1. The accumulation of scientific knowledge is a gradual process that often follows the path of "two steps forward and one step back." Show how this is true of topics discussed in this chapter.

2. In Japan, social control over behavior is an important theme and very young children may be disciplined for misbehavior with admonitions like, "How do you think it makes our guests feel when you make a mess at the table?" In view of information contained in this chapter, what affect is this likely to have on a preschool child?

3. Why do you think that adult forms of humor--puns, for example--have no effect on preschool children?

ANSWERS WITH PAGE REFERENCES

Fill in the Blanks

1. preoperational (291)
   egocentric (291)
2. objective (291)
   do not (291)
3. Flavell (292)
4. decenter (293)
   conservation (293)
   appearances (294)
   reality (294)
5. intellectual realism
      (294)
   phenomenism (294)
6. Pretense (295)
7. four (296)
   one-to-one
      correspondence (296)
   cardinality rule (296)
   order irrelevancy (296)
8. metacognition (299)

9. intelligence (300)
   valid (300)
   validity (300)
   school (300)
10. Binet and Simon (300)
    intelligence quotient
       (301)
    mental age (301)
    chronological age (301)
    100 (301)
11. adults (301)
12. Stanford Binet (301)
    WISC (301)
    WPPSI (302)
13. reliable (304)
    error of measurement
       (303)
14. disadvantaged (305)
    temporary (305)

15.	200 or 300 (306)	20.	innate (312)
	2500 (306)		retarded (312)
16.	Fast mapping (306)		brain-damaged (312)
17.	class-inclusion (307)		environment (313)
18.	typical (308)	21.	active (313)
19.	grammatical		first-born (314)
	morphemes (310)		first-born (315)
	complexity (311)		parents (315)
			brothers and sisters (315)
		22.	private speech (316)
			regulate (316)

Multiple Choice

1.	B (291)	9.	C (294)	17.	B (301)	25.	B (312)
2.	C (291)	10.	B (294)	18.	C (303)	26.	D (315, 317)
3.	C (291)	11.	A (296)	19.	B (304)		
4.	B (293)	12.	A (296)	20.	D (302)	27.	D (314)
5.	A (293)	13.	B (296)	21.	B (304)	28.	A (316)
6.	D (291)	14.	A (300)	22.	A (310)	29.	C (308)
7.	D (296)	15.	C (301)	23.	D (306)	30.	C (312)
8.	B (299)	16.	A (299)	24.	D (306)		

SUGGESTED ANSWERS TO THOUGHT QUESTIONS

1. Jean Piaget was for years considered to be the foremost
    authority on the cognitive development of children, and his
    theories were viewed as the best explanation of that
    development. Learning programs for children were based on
    those theories. Now, however, it has been discovered that
    in some respects Piaget was incorrect in his conclusions.
    Children seem to show evidence of advanced thought
    processes earlier than Piaget suspected, and some of the
    shortcomings of children's thinking may be due to causes
    that Piaget did not recognize. In any case, psychologists
    are now having to rethink the process of cognitive
    development in children because we know less about it than
    we thought we did. In the end, though, as a result of new
    research, we will know more.

2. Very young children have difficulty taking another person's
    point of view, even in fairly concrete things such as
    visual displays. It would probably be even more difficult
    for them to imagine others' emotional responses to their
    behavior. So for a three- or four-year old, such
    admonitions probably have little of the intended effect,
    although the child may get the message that the behavior in
    question is disapproved of. Since the parents stress this
    approach to discipline continuously, however, when the
    child finally is capable of grasping the concept, he will

103

learn it quickly. As a result, Japanese children probably have a greater sense of other people's reactions to their behavior than Western children do, since in our culture this attitude may not be taught until some time after the child is capable of grasping it, and even then it may not be emphasized to any great degree.

3. In the preschool stages of language acquisition, children tend to be very concrete about their use of words. They have trouble with classes and subconcepts within classes, for example. As a result, plays on words would be far beyond the preschooler's ability to comprehend.

Chapter 10

Becoming a Member of Society

AN OVERVIEW OF THE CHAPTER

Chapter 10 describes some of the forces working during the preschool period that shape the child into a member of society. As they grow, children must learn what the rules of society are, and they must learn to make themselves follow those rules since they are now spending less time under close adult supervision.

The chapter describes the impact of three major parenting styles, and discusses some important issues in childrearing. The use of punishment and how to deal with the physically aggressive child are two of these issues. The teaching of self-control and the delay of gratification are two more parental concerns, because these are critical skills for the child to possess if he is to lead a successful adult life.

Research suggests that prosocial behaviors (sharing, cooperating and helping) may not have to be actively taught as long as the child is not exposed to models who actively demonstrate a lack of concern for others. However, according to another study mentioned in the text, modeling prosocial behavior can't hurt: "...mothers who are helpful and sympathetic toward their children tend to have helpful and sympathetic children."

The sex role that one has in society influences how one thinks and behaves. The chapter explores how children get sex-role knowledge and take on gender identities for themselves. How much of the process is biochemically determined by hormones and how much is learned are major concerns.

Play is discussed in this chapter because it is the process through which the child practices his social skills with his peers. Types of play can be defined by how much interaction with other children is involved. Play is the "work" of the child; through it he experiments with the environment without serious consequences, and pretends at what he wants to be. He may use fantasy play to resolve emotional stress. Play is also the arena in which children learn to develop friendships. Imaginary playmates seem to be the creative child's response to the need for companionship. Lying is also dealt with here because separating it from fantasy play is a challenge for both the parent and for the cognitive skills of the young child.

There is a special interest box about autism. Autism is a rare and severe disorder that is probably caused by a physical abnormality of the brain resulting from a genetic factor. Autistic children are unresponsive to the forces of socialization. They do not make eye contact, and they are unlikely to attach to any person. They have an intense desire for things in the environment to always stay just the same. They may engage in simple repetitive behaviors for hours. If they learn to talk, their use of the language will be limited and very primitive in nature.

KEY TERMS AND CONCEPTS

infantile autism
autistic
internalize
authoritarian
authoritative
permissive
delay of gratification
prosocial behavior
sex-role development
gender identity
sex roles
sex-role knowledge

sex stereotypes
sex constancy
sex-typed behavior
solitary play
onlooker behavior
parallel play
associative play
cooperative play
sociodramatic play
social pretend play

CHAPTER OBJECTIVES--CHECK YOURSELF
By the time you've finished reading and studying this chapter, you should be able to:

1. Describe three important changes that occur as toddlers become preschoolers.

2. Describe the lack of socialization that the autistic child demonstrates.

3. Explain the three major patterns of parenting and describe the type of child that each produces.

4. Explain the transactional reinterpretation of Baumrind's conclusion and the very destructive "vicious circle" between parent and child that it explains.

5. Explain how the family under stress is likely to also come under the additional stress of parent-child problems.

6. List types of punishments that parents can use and describe the relationship between physical punishments and aggressiveness in children.

7. List the guidelines for parenting an aggressive child.

8. Explain the importance of the child learning self-control and delay of gratification, and describe the method for teaching these skills that is advocated by the authors.

9. Describe the development of prosocial behaviors.

10. List and explain the different aspects of sex-role development.

11. Explain the suggested causes of sex-typed behavior, including the conclusions drawn from the case study of the identical twins who were "opposite sexed."

12. Explain the major factor that seems to underlie gender differences.

13. List Parten's and Piaget's categories of play and the purposes that play serves for the child.

14. Discuss the use of fantasy by children.

15. Discuss the preschooler's behavior in making friends.

REVIEW EXERCISE--FILL IN THE BLANKS

1. The change from toddler to preschooler brings more _____ from Mom and less _____ with her. _____ attached children seem to do better at developing this distance from Mom.

2. The child's first step in learning to govern himself as he _____ parental rules is often saying the rules _____ .

3. In autism, we see the failure to _____ and become _____. Autistic children seek _____ in their environments and engage in _____ behaviors, some of which can even be self-destructive. Autism seems to be caused by a _____ abnormality, probably in the _____ side.

4. _____ parents follow the "traditional" viewpoint: obedience is a virtue, and children are to be seen and not heard. Their children tend to be _____ achievement motivated and _____ independent, which is similar to the children raised by _____ parents.

5. Permissive parents give their children as much _____ as possible and put _____ demands on them.

6. _____ parents listen to their children's opinions and take them into consideration, but the final decision belongs to the parents. These parents turn out children who are the most _____, _____, _____, and _____.

7. As in chapter 7 with cognitive development, parental _____ seems to be a critical factor in parenting, and whether the interactions are _____ or _____ in tone is also important.

8. In the transactional reinterpretation of parenting, the parent-child relationship may be the result of the interaction of the parents' _____ and the child's _____.

9. Families under stress are the least likely to use an authoritative parenting style because they lack the _____ and _____ to set _____ and enforce them.

10. Harsh physical punishment may temporarily suppress _____, particularly in the presence of the _____. However, in the long run it is counterproductive because children who experience harsh physical punishment are more likely to be _____. This pattern can become a(n) _____ of escalating violence.

11. _____ is best prevented by not letting the child get into situations that are past his _____ tolerance. Modeling _____ conflict resolution and _____ the child when he uses these behaviors will teach him needed skills. Parents also need to make sure that the child is not gaining some kind of _____ for engaging in the aggressive behaviors.

12. Learning to _____ one's emotional behaviors and to be able to _____ gratification are two major steps toward being responsible, socially adept, and able to cope with _____.

13. The helping behaviors, which include sharing, cooperation, and helpfulness, are called _____ behaviors. These behaviors are so commonly seen in children of _____ ages, that teaching the behaviors may be unnecessary as long as the child has not learned the opposite by seeing examples of distinctly _____ behaviors.

14. Seeing behaviors modeled is not always necessary; _____ can be quite effective for teaching.

15. Society's expectations of people of each sex are known as _____. They encompass _____, _____, and _____. When they are rigidly defined, they are called _____.

16. About age _____ years, the child starts to know his own gender. This is called the child's _____. When the child learns that gender is determined by genitals, and that

108

changing clothes and hair style does not affect one's sex, the child has developed _____.

17. Most detectable sex differences in early childhood are _____. The one that leads to sex segregation among children is level of _____, which is probably caused by _____. By age _____ years, girls tend to be dominated by boys.

18. Play enables young organisms to _____ many of the skills they will need as they grow older.

19. _____ play involves no interaction with other children. In _____ play, a child watches other children play. In _____ play, two or more children are engaged in the same activity but there seems to be no awareness of the activity of the other. In _____ play, there seems to be more awareness of the presence of the other, but there is still no effort to integrate their independent playing. Organized play interactions toward a common goal is _____ play.

20. Piaget's categories of play are _____, _____, and _____.

21. Sometimes playing out _____ in fantasy form may give children a way of dealing with them, although it may also intensify them.

PRACTICE EXAM

1. Preschoolers use private speech to _____.
   A. get attention from their mothers
   B. get attention from people who do not know them
   C. try to help themselves control their own behaviors
   D. engage in fantasy play with imaginary playmates

2. One of the symptoms of an autistic child is _____.
   A. hearing imaginary voices
   B. failing to make eye contact with other people
   C. having more than one imaginary playmate
   D. compulsive lying

3. The autistic child will be the most upset by _____.
   A. having to move to a new house
   B. wearing the same shirt two days in a row
   C. having to entertain himself for 15 minutes
   D. being left in the care of his father

4. A child who self-regulates behavior based on his parents' rules of behavior _____.
   A. is using sociodrama
   B. is delaying gratification until he leaves home
   C. is fulfilling his role in prosocial schema
   D. has internalized parental standards

5. In terms of parenting styles, the two groups of children that are most similar are those raised by _____.
    A. authoritative and authoritarian parents
    B. authoritative and permissive parents
    C. authoritarian and permissive parents
    D. prosocial and permissive parents

6. The style of childrearing which results in the most independent, successful child is _____.
    A. authoritarian   C. prosocial
    B. authoritative   D. permissive

7. In the transactional view of parent-child relationships, _____ are seen contributing to the nature of the interactions.
    A. the parents' discipline techniques alone
    B. the child's characteristics alone
    C. the parent's and child's reactions to each other
    D. sociodramatics

8. To use the authoritative approach to parenting, one needs _____.
    A. training in child psychology
    B. time and energy
    C. a strong religious faith
    D. a single-parent family environment

9. According to your text, parents who have normal (not unusually troublesome) kids tend to adhere to the principle that discipline should be _____.
    A. administered before the lecture and scolding
    B. administered on an intermittent basis
    C. the result of a parent-child compromise
    D. tailored to fit the misbehavior

10. The difference between abusive and nonabusive parents was: _____.
    A. nonabusive parents reported using physical punishment less than once a month
    B. nonabusive parents used more isolation techniques for discipline measures
    C. abusive parents used more of all types of punishments
    D. abusive parents used more permissiveness between punishments

11. Letting your child hit a punching bag _____.
    A. will help him release some of his aggressive energy
    B. may increase the likelihood that he will behave aggressively in other situations
    C. seems to have the same end effect as reasoning
    D. will increase self-control skills for aggression

12. According to your text, aggression is most frequently observed in children who _____.
    A. have been subjected to harsh physical punishment
    B. have had permissive parenting
    C. are autistic
    D. are prosocial

13. Parents of aggressive children should _____.
    A. use milder physical punishments
    B. use frustration inducing techniques
    C. reinforce behaviors that are incompatible with aggression
    D. encourage children to use up their aggression through fantasy

14. Many American children have to learn public self-control of emotional behavior earlier because _____.
    A. they go to nursery schools
    B. their parents use authoritative parenting methods
    C. they internalize parents' rules and regulations earlier
    D. they mature earlier cognitively

15. The vicious circle of escalating violence in the parent-child relationship results when _____.
    A. parents use a permissive parenting style
    B. parents use physical punishment
    C. parents reinforce children for nonviolence
    D. parents allow children to watch violence on television

16. Tommy is aggressive when he visits at his grandmother's house. His aggressiveness is most likely caused by _____.
    A. his parents not letting him be aggressive at home
    B. his grandmother laughingly saying "you're all boy" when she disciplines his aggressiveness
    C. his grandmother's refusal to spank Tommy for his aggressiveness
    D. his grandmother's treating him like a baby

17. The best way to deal with aggressive behavior is to _____.
    A. use a mildly painful physical punishment
    B. withdraw affection
    C. ignore it
    D. prevent it

18. Ability to delay gratification closely relates to the ability to _____.
    A. acquire sex-role knowledge
    B. manipulate permissive parents
    C. develop friendships
    D. resist temptations

19. Sex-typed behavior and sex-role knowledge _____.
    A. are directly related
    B. are indirectly related
    C. are conversely related
    D. do not appear to depend on each other

20. Gender constancy means the child _____.
    A. has made a permanent gender identification
    B. learns to ignore sex stereotypes
    C. knows that gender is based on genitals
    D. still thinks that mamas and daddies can both
       have babies (be pregnant)

21. Sex-typed behaviors are those considered appropriate
    for _____.
    A. each sex
    B. courting couples to engage in publicly without social
       censure
    C. people who have reached the age of consent
    D. private moments only

22. Adults judge preschoolers' facial expressions to reflect
    specific emotions depending on _____.
    A. whether the mother is present
    B. what kind of play the child was engaging in
    C. the age of the child
    D. the sex of the child

23. In mixed-sex interactions at age 2 1/2 years, one can
    expect to see dominance by _____.
    A. the boys
    B. the girls
    C. the children who are physically the largest
    D. the children who are the most verbal

24. In "The Case of the Opposite-sexed Identical Twin" the
    doctors seem to think _____.
    A. the double standard should apply
    B. a "wrong" sex is better than no sex at all
    C. tomboyish girls are cute
    D. hormone therapy is insufficient for sexual
       reidentification

25. The type of play where two or more children will take part
    in the same activity, all doing basically the same thing,
    but where there is no attempt to organize the activity or
    to take turns is called _____.
    A. associative play   C. cooperative play
    B. parallel play   D. solitary play

26. In Piagetian theory, the earliest kind of play is _____.
    A. circular reactionistic play
    B. sensorimotor play
    C. pretend play
    D. sociodramatic play

27. Solitary and social pretend play both tend to peak about age _____ years.
A. 3   B. 5   C. 7   D. 9

28. Around the age of _____ years, the importance of truth should be emphasized to the child.
A. 1-2   B. 3-4   C. 5-6   D. 7-8

29. In a laboratory experiment with white rats, baby rats that were taken out of their cages and subjected to stressful experiences _____.
A. developed abnormally
B. turned out to be a little smaller physically
C. grew up to be more fearful and excitable than rats who had not been stressed
D. were able to cope well with stress as adults

30. Preschoolers tend to choose as friends _____.
A. children of the same age and gender
B. children who have more advanced play styles
C. older children of the same sex
D. younger children of the opposite sex

THOUGHT QUESTIONS

1. What are some sex-typed behaviors that have changed in recent years for men?

2. What would you have done if you had been the parent of the baby boy who was left without a penis after an accident?

3. What type parenting style did your parents use? (Assign percentages of each style that you experienced if there was a mixture, or if one parent used one and the other parent used another).

4. What type of parenting style did you, or do you intend to, use with your own children?

5. What punishments did your parents use with you? Do you consider your parents to have ever been abusive and if so, in what way?

ANSWERS WITH PAGE REFERENCES

Fill in the Blanks

1. distance (321)
   interaction (321)
   securely (321)
2. internalizes (321)
   aloud (321)
3. attach (322)
   socialized (322)
   sameness (322)
   repetitive (322)
   brain (323)
   left (323)

4. Authoritarian (322)
   less (323)
   less (323)
   permissive (323)
5. freedom (323)
   few (322)
6. Authoritative (322)
   responsible (323)
   assertive (323)
   self-reliant (323)
   friendly (323)
7. responsiveness (324)
   positive (324)
   negative (324)
8. parenting style (325)
   characteristics (325)
9. time (326)
   energy (326)
   limits (326)
10. aggression(329)
    punishing adult (329)
    aggressive (327)
    vicious circle (328)
11. aggression (331)
    frustration (331)
    nonviolent (331)
    reinforcing (331)
    reinforcement (331)

12. control (332)
    delay (332)
    frustration (332)
13. prosocial (333)
    all (333)
    uncaring (333)
14. verbal instruction (333)
15. sex roles (334)
    attitudes (334)
    behaviors (334)
    psychological
      characteristics (334)
    sex stereotypes (334)
16. two (334)
    gender identity (334)
    sex constancy (334)
17. small (340)
    aggression (340)
    hormones (340)
    2 1/2 (340)
18. practice (343)
19. solitary (341)
    onlooker (342)
    parallel (342)
    associative (342)
    cooperative (342)
20. sensorimotor (342)
    pretend (342)
    social pretend (342)
21. fears (334)

Multiple Choice

1.	C (320)	9.	D (327)	17.	D (331)	25.	A (342)
2.	B (322)	10.	C (327)	18.	D (332)	26.	B (342)
3.	A (322)	11.	B (329)	19.	D (336)	27.	B (343)
4.	D (321)	12.	A (327)	20.	C (334)	28.	B (345)
5.	C (323)	13.	C (330)	21.	A (336)	29.	D (344)
6.	B (323)	14.	A (331)	22.	D (337)	30.	A (347)
7.	C (325)	15.	B (328)	23.	A (339)		
8.	B (326)	16.	B (331)	24.	B (336)		

SUGGESTED ANSWERS TO THOUGHT QUESTIONS

1. Men are now using blow dryers, hair spray, and styling gels
   on their hair. Men are now wearing earrings in one ear.
   This is recently new, but was seen in pirates centuries
   ago. Men and women are now working in non-traditional
   jobs. Women are on highway work crews and men are more
   frequently becoming nurses and secretaries than they have
   in past years.

2.   You could choose to do what the parents in your text elected to do. Another possibility would be to raise the boy as a male without a penis, explaining to him that it takes more than a penis to make a man. Assuming that he had at least one of his testicles still intact, he could still have grown up to be a reproductive male with the use of artificial insemination. Even if the boy had no hormone-producing testicular tissue left, he could have been given male hormones so that his body would have developed into a normal looking adult male body when clothed. Another question to be considered is what, if any, neurological tissue was still present to allow for a satisfactory means of sexual gratification later in life.

3.   The three types described in the chapter are authoritarian, authoritative, and permissive.

4.   Same choices as described in Answer 3.

5.   Possible punishments are isolation, withdrawal of privileges, fines, verbal attack (You're bad or stupid). name calling (Idiot!), or physical punishment.
     Abuse is that which endangers the child's mental or physical wellbeing.

Chapter 11

The School-Age Child

AN OVERVIEW OF THE CHAPTER

Chapter 11 focuses on "middle childhood," ages 6 to 12 years. Although these are important years in the life of the child, they are relatively calm ones. Physical growth is comparatively slow. There are however, striking changes in intellectual competence and in relationships with others.

School-age children are taller, leaner, and more muscular than preschoolers. There are individual differences in development, however, and these individual differences (in appearance, intellectual abilities, talents, inclinations, and so on) show up clearly during middle childhood. Although girls are physically more mature than boys, boys surpass them in most measures of athletic ability and strength.

According to Piaget, the preoperational period gives way to the period of concrete operations around the age of 7. The important advances in cognitive development that take place between the ages of 5 and 7 prepare the child for first grade. What they learn in school leads, in turn, to more cognitive development.

The child's advance in metacognitive skills is a major reason for his growth in cognitive competence. One source of this development is the child's increasing ability to use words and symbols to serve a variety of metacognitive functions. Words serve as "verbal mediators": a stimulus sets off the verbal mediator, which then sets off the child's response. The use of verbal mediators to learn or remember something is a "metacognitive strategy."

Information-processing theorists vary in their views of cognitive development, but all see their approaches in contrast to Piaget's. They also agree in depicting the human mind as a set of components that function more or less independently and that work by following a set of instructions, like a computer program.

Memory was the first aspect of human cognition to be given an information-processing interpretation. Two main "hardware" components have been defined: short-term memory and long-term memory. Short-term memory can hold only a few items at a time, and only for as long as they are rehearsed. Memory span increases gradually from about three items at the age of 3 to six or seven items in adulthood. Items in long-term memory have always been in short-term memory first, but not all items in short-term memory are put into long-term memory. Older children are better than younger children at memory retrieval; this is probably due to better memory organization.

The chapter also contains a discussion of the problems of "bed-wetting," childhood obesity, and the issue of "Where Do Babies Come From?"

KEY TERMS AND CONCEPTS

middle childhood	short-term memory
peer group	long-term memory
set-point weight	memory span
period of concrete operations	information processing
animism	encoding
artificialism	memory retrieval
discrimination task	recall
verbal mediator	recognition
metacognitive strategy	scripts
elaboration	selective attention

CHAPTER OBJECTIVES--CHECK YOURSELF

By the time you've finished reading and studying this chapter, you should be able to:

1. Describe the physical changes that usually occur in middle childhood.

2. Identify the differences between boys and girls with respect to athletic ability.

3. Describe the implications of the Weisfeld study of mixed-sex competition in dodge-ball.

4. List the percentage of bed-wetters per age group. Discuss the cause of enuresis, and the most effective treatment.

5. Describe the changes that occur in intellectual development as the child moves from preoperational thought to concrete operational thought.

6. List some of the concepts that children master that increase their knowledge and understanding of the world.

7. State what the "American question" is and give its answer.

8. Explain what a metacognitive skill is and list some of these skills that children use.

9. Explain the information-processing view of cognitive development.

10. Compare and contrast the information-processing view of cognitive development and the approach taken by Piaget.

11. Describe the relationship between memory and selective attention and explain how this relationship changes with age.

12. Compare and contrast Piaget's theory and Siegler's theory on children's problem solving strategies.

HELPFUL HINT

This chapter has introduced you to the concept of metacognition, if you were previously unaware of it. This introduction can be an important beginning for the improvement of **your** metacognitive skills. You can analyze your approaches to problem solving, thinking, and memory to find which strategies you already happen to be using and to what degree. You can develop those that are helpful to you and you can pursue information to discover new ones. Look for information about cognition and metacognitive strategies at your college library. You should now recognize previously dismissed pamphlets on study skills and on the use of mnemonic devices as valuable sources of information on enhancing your metacognitive strategies.

REVIEW EXERCISE--FILL IN THE BLANKS

1. Middle childhood covers ages _____. Children enter middle childhood looking and acting much more _____ to one another than when they leave it. _____ differences show up clearly during middle childhood.

2. The most frequent threat to a child's life during this period of life is from _____, particularly those involving _____. Diseases of earlier years are no longer rampant, but there is the danger that parents will neglect _____.

3. Sex differences in height and weight at age 6 years are _____. By age 11 or 12 the average _____ is taller and heavier than the average _____. _____ are ahead in measures of athletic ability and strength. Girls' performances level off where boys' performances continue to _____ dramatically.

4. Obesity is a(n) _____ problem in the U.S. There is a _____ factor in obesity because children are found to be more like their birth parents than their adopted parents. Television is an _____ factor that encourages obesity because it reduces _____ and is paired with _____.

5. According to Piaget, the period of _____ operations begins around the age of 7. Piaget admitted that is possible to _____ cognitive development; however, he said the _____ must still be followed. The issue of whether or not to speed up cognitive development is _____.

6. Piaget did not think preschoolers could consider more than one aspect of a situation at a time. That is, they were unable to _____. He believed they were _____ in that they could not consider the point of view of another. The school-age child progressively masters these tasks.

7. The school age child is acquiring much information. He no longer believes that anything that moves or does something is alive. That is, he no longer believes in _____. He understands the concept of death by age _____ years.

8. When left to their own intellectual devices, children tend to answer the question "Where did I come from?" with man-made solutions, or _____. Their most ready source of information on the topic seems to be _____.

9. Level of humor reflects _____ level of development, particularly _____ comprehension. Preschool humor is based on _____. Joke-telling tends to decline near the _____ of middle childhood.

10. Thinking about how to think more efficiently is working on your _____ skills. Verbal _____ is one of these skills; it means talking to _____ to help you solve a problem. The term mediator is used because it works between the _____ and the _____.

11. A metacognitive strategy that is useful for linking two words together in memory is called _____. A technique used in remembering a list of items by grouping them into similar classes is called _____.

12. Information-processing theorists see the mind like a _____. _____ was the first area of cognition considered in this way.

13. Memory is divided into _____ and _____. Unlike visual memory which peaks about age _____ years, both of these types of memory tend to _____ with age.

14. Short-term memory has _____ capacity. The number of items that can be held in short-term memory is called _____. Information is usually maintained in short-term memory by _____.

15. Processing a stimulus so that it has some meaningfulness is called _____. The term would seem to suggest that you are putting it into a code that is usable to you.

16. There are two types of memory tests discussed in this chapter: _____ is when you must find the memory without external cues. In a _____ test, cues are given and you must pick out the correct one.

17. Memories of events that are quite similar may be organized into general patterns called _____.

18. The ability to focus on what is important and ignore that which is not important is called _____. This is very important in developing a good _____.

PRACTICE EXAM

1. Which of the following does not occur during middle childhood?
   A. rapid physical growth
   B. increasing intellectual competence
   C. changes in relationships with adults and other children
   D. dramatic increase in the fund of knowledge that the child has

2. Which of the following physical characteristics are typical of a child in middle childhood?
   A. top-heavy look   C. short legs
   B. big front teeth   D. chubby cheeks

3. In middle childhood the most frequent threat to a child's life is _____.
   A. measles   C. accidents
   B. inoculations   D. rheumatic fever

4. Which is of the following is a sex difference between boys and girls in middle childhood?
   A. Boys are heavier and taller than girls by age 11.
   B. Girls are two years closer to physical maturity than boys at age 12.
   C. Boys are slower runners at age 11 than are girls.
   D. Girls are slightly better ball-throwers at age 11 than are boys.

5. Girls persistently lag behind boys in _____.
   A. height
   B. weight
   C. strength
   D. eye-hand coordination

6. According to a replay analysis, the girls always lost in
   the dodge-ball games against boys because _____.
   A. the boys play unfairly
   B. the boys use verbal intimidation
   C. the highly skilled girl players refused to play against
      the skilled boy players
   D. the girls became less competitive when playing against
      boys

7. At about age 7 years, children _____.
   A. stop decentering
   B. move into formal operational thinking
   C. enter the period of concrete operations
   D. develop egocentrism

8. The "American question" refers to _____.
   A. how girls lose their competitive spirit in mix-
      sexed games
   B. whether cognitive development can be accelerated
   C. whether there should be sex education in public schools
   D. what to do about the obese child

9. According to one theory, humor in children is usually
   related to their _____.
   A. mood   C. ability to decenter
   B. egocentrism   D. level of cognitive development

10. Children at the age of 7 or 8 are likely to _____.
    A. believe in animism
    B. believe their dreams are real
    C. understand that death is permanent cessation of all
       functions
    D. be skillful in problems based on time

11. With respect to speeding up cognitive development, Piaget
    himself felt that it _____.
    A. was not possible
    B. was possible if stages were skipped
    C. was possible, but that the order of the stages would
       have to be altered
    D. was possible, but all stages would still have to be
       followed in sequence

12. Enrichment programs for children from impoverished
    environments should include _____.
    A. instruction in anti-animism theory
    B. experience in working within a time schedule
    C. exposure to middle-class humor
    D. metacognitive therapy

13. A third grade teacher notices that one of her students
    tells jokes that are usually based on funny sounds or
    the mislabeling of common objects with nonsense names; the
    teacher concludes that _____.
    A. the child is gifted
    B. the child is from an impoverished environment
    C. the child's cognitive development is delayed
    D. the child skipped the preoperational cognitive stage

14. An example of an artificial explanation for where
    babies come from is: _____.
    A. they are made from modelling clay by the nurses at the
       hospital
    B. they float down on a cloud from heaven
    C. they form in the dew under cabbage leaves
    D. they grow from germs in the mother's stomach

15. In research on discrimination tasks, _____.
    A. verbal mediators interfered with task solution
    B. verbal mediators were helpful
    C. visual memory was enhanced
    D. visual memory replaced rehearsal techniques

16. Deliberately using verbal mediators to help increase
    your memory in studying for a test would be _____.
    A. regression to a preoperational level
    B. decentering for cognitive advantage
    C. a metacognitive strategy
    D. a vocal discriminator task

17. When you are developing elaborations on ideas to enhance
    your memory, you should _____.
    A. keep them simple
    B. make them short
    C. make them vivid
    D. avoid crossed connections

18. Which of the following is NOT a metacognitive skill?
    A. conservation of length
    B. discussing a problem with one's self
    C. rehearsal
    D. deliberately focusing one's attention to enhance
       retention

19. Information processing sees the mind as being like a(n)
    _____.
    A. typewriter   C. camera
    B. sponge   D. computer

20. Which of the following is NOT true about short-term memory?
    A. It has limited capacity.
    B. All information in long-term memory has been in short-term memory at some point.
    C. All information in short-term memory will go into long-term memory.
    D. Verbal rehearsal is a useful technique to enhance short-term memory.

21. A neurological phenomenon that is likely very important to the increasing skill and speed of information processing is _____.
    A. myelination
    B. scripting
    C. an increase in the set point
    D. the increase in the number of neurons in middle childhood

22. Which of the following are the three processes of memory?
    A. retrieval, recall, recognition
    B. encoding, storage, retrieval
    C. recognition, metacognition, production
    D. metacognition, storage, recall

23. A 3-year-old's short-term memory span is about _____ items.
    A. 1   B. 3   C. 7   D. 11

24. An adult's short-term memory span is generally about _____ items.
    A. 3   B. 7   C. 11   D. 15

25. A way of organizing memories to take advantage of the fact that many of the things that happen to people are very similar to things that have happened before, relates to the concept of _____.
    A. elaboration   C. rehearsal
    B. centering   D. scripts

26. Robert Siegler of Carnegie Mellon University believes that children who cannot solve the conservation problems where water is poured from one size and shaped glass to another of different proportion have a problem with _____.
    A. encoding relevant information
    B. decentering
    C. metacognitive strategies
    D. short-term memory

27. When taking a test of memory, which of the following types of test is the easiest?
    A. recall   C. retrieval
    B. rehearsal   D. recognition

28. Selective attention means your attention _____.
    A. is focused on some topic but not on others
    B. always goes to your favorite topics
    C. is on a metacognitive task
    D. is in a problem solving mode

29. If you are taking college algebra, you probably _____.
    A. retrieve your multiplication tables from long-term memory
    B. retrieve your multiplication tables from short-term memory
    C. use a backup calculation strategy to get your multiplication tables
    D. use a metacognitive strategy to retrieve your multiplication tables

30. Siegler and Piaget agree on one point, which is: _____.
    A. All stages are mastered in the end.
    B. Adaptation to the environment is the final result.
    C. Category elaboration should be the ultimate goal.
    D. Average children ultimately adjust the best.

THOUGHT QUESTIONS

1. If you were the activities director at an after-school child care center, how would the results of the Weisfeld study affect your programming?

2. What could explain the knowledge that present-day American children have about living things and inanimate objects?

3. List some of the metacognitive strategies that you use.

4. What information in this chapter suggests an area where adults and children can compete as equals?

ANSWERS WITH PAGE REFERENCES

Fill in the Blanks

1. 6-12 years (350)
   similar (351)
   Individual (351)
2. accidents (354)
   automobiles (354)
   inoculations (353)
3. negligible (355)
   girl (355)
   boy (355)
   Boys (355)
   improve (355)

4. increasing (352)
   genetic (352)
   environmental (352)
   exercise (352)
   snacking (352)
5. concrete (357)
   accelerate (367)
   order of stages (367)
   unclear (367)
6. decenter (357)
   egocentric (358)

7. animism (359)
    6-7 (361)
8. artificialism (364)
    older siblings (365)
9. cognitive (363)
    verbal (363)
    silliness (363)
    end (365)
10. metacognition (367)
    mediation (367)
    yourself (367)
    stimulus (368)
    response (368)
11. elaboration (371)
    categorization (371)
12. computer (373)
    memory (373)
13. long-term (373)
    short-term (373)
    five (370)
    increase (374-75)
14. limited (373)
    memory span (374)
    rehearsal (373)
15. encoding (374)
16. recall (375)
    recognition (375)
17. scripts (376)
18. selective attention
       (377)
    memory (377)

Multiple Choice

1.	A (350)	9.	D (363)	17.	C (371)	25.	D (376)
2.	B (351)	10.	C (361)	18.	A (367)	26.	A (377)
3.	C (354)	11.	D (367)	19.	D (373)	27.	D (375)
4.	B (355)	12.	B (362)	20.	C (375)	28.	A (377)
5.	C (355)	13.	C (363)	21.	A (375)	29.	A (375)
6.	D (356)	14.	A (364)	22.	B (374)	30.	B (378)
7.	C (357)	15.	B (368)	23.	B (374)		
8.	B (366)	16.	C (368)	24.	B (374)		

SUGGESTED ANSWERS TO THOUGHT QUESTIONS

1. The Weisfeld results suggest several possible courses of
    action:
    a. Whatever sports activities were used would be designed
        to be as noncompetitive as possible.
    b. Separate sports competitions would be held for boys
        and girls, or
    c. Individual teams could be mix-sexed to see if girls
        would compete in that circumstance.
    d. Girls could be given a pep rally experience before
        competition with males to try to motivate them to
        actively compete against the boys, and
    d. Enticing incentives could be given to the winners to
        increase motivation for active competition.

2. Since Piaget's study was based on his three children (see
    Chapter 3, page 96), perhaps that was one area his children
    had not experienced as much as other children; however,
    since Piaget was a biologist, that seems unlikely.
        Another possibility is that present-day American
    children are more educated on the subject through exposure

to the many television science programs for children, particularly on the public broadcasting network.

3. Here are some possible metacognitive strategies:
    A. Techniques to motivate and direct your attention
        a. sitting closer to the front of the classroom
        b. rewarding yourself for good study periods
        c. meditating to clear the mind before beginning study
    B. Techniques to enhance concept formation
        a. using private talk to question yourself about how much understanding you have and where it stops, so you can start at your first weak point, or at the biggest problem area, or wherever you judge to be the best starting point
        b. drawing diagrams
        c. attending study groups to be stimulated by the other students' cognitions
        d. reading other texts to see the same material discussed in another author's words
    C. Techniques to improve memory of understood concepts
        a. rehearsal--write them, sing them, or say them
        b. elaborate them and devise mnemonic devices
        c. categorize concepts into hierarchical patterns

4. Games based on visual memory would allow 5- and 6-years olds to play as equals against college students, according to the the text. Having had this experience myself, be prepared as an adult to genuinely lose to a youngster.

Chapter 12

The Child in School

Chapter Twelve introduces us to the main career of middle
childhood: learning in school. This activity is extremely
important because the child who does well in school will
probably lead a very different kind of adult life than the child
who does poorly. Some of the qualities that are required for
success in school are the ability to concentrate on something
despite distractions, the motivation to do well, and
intelligence. IQ scores have been found to correlate highly
with academic success.

Other factors affecting achievement are creativity,
cultural attitudes toward education, differences in personality,
differences in cognitive style, parental encouragement, the type
of school environment, and teacher expectancy. Your text also
discusses gender differences in school achievement and the needs
of children in the gifted and retarded categories.

In the early years of learning arithmetic, easy problems
are solved from memory; more difficult ones are solved by
counting. Young children are less likely to make a mistake if
they are permitted to count on their fingers. Fewer mistakes,
in turn, hastens the time when they can reliably depend on
memory for the correct answers. Cultural differences in math
achievement may not only involve general attitudes toward
education but also the way a given culture deals with numbers in
its language. Several Asian cultures, for example, have
languages that speak of numbers in a way that is less confusing
than in English. The effect of calculators and computers in the
classroom is also discussed.

Reading is the most important skill a child acquires in
school. Some people never learn to read. Children who are
unable to divide spoken words into their separate sounds are
likely to have trouble learning to read well. There has been
much controversy surrounding the teaching of reading. Although
most children learn to read regardless of the teaching method,

127

those who are taught phonics from the start tend to be better readers.

The chapter includes special sections on learning disabilities and on the effect a dedicated teacher can have on her students.

KEY TERMS AND CONCEPTS

educable mentally retarded
organic retardation
cultural-familial retardation
mental retardation
visual-spatial ability
divergent thinking
impulsive
reflective
achievement motivation
intrinsic motivation
extrinsic motivation
performance goal
learning goal

internal locus of control
external locus of control
mastery oriented
self-efficacy
self-fulfilling prophecy
whole-word method
sight-reading method
phonics
dyslexic
learning disability
dyslexia
attention deficit disorder
     with hyperactivity (ADD-H)

CHAPTER OBJECTIVES--CHECK YOURSELF

By the time you've finished reading and studying this chapter, you should be able to:

1. Explain why school performance is important for the future life of a child.

2. Discuss the relationship between IQ scores and achievement in school.

3. Compare and contrast familial and organic mental retardation.

4. Summarize research examining the differences in IQ scores and school performance among different ethnic groups.

5. Summarize research examining gender differences in IQ scores and school performance.

6. Discuss parenting style as it affects school performance.

7. Compare the styles of impulsive and reflective children and discuss the implications these styles have for school success.

8. Explain the difference between intrinsic and extrinsic motivation and summarize the effects of each.

9. Explain the difference between a performance goal and a learning goal orientation, and summarize the effects of each.

10. List three dimensions of performance attribution and explain how they relate to each other.

11. List characteristics of schools that contribute to student success.

12. Describe how good teachers influence their students' achievements.

13. Compare the achievements of students in open, informal classrooms to those in traditional, formal classrooms.

14. Summarize arguments for and against finger counting in young children learning math, and state the results of recent research on the issue.

15. Discuss the pros and cons of calculators and computers in the classroom.

16. Cite several explanations for the superiority of first and second generation Asian Americans in the area of math.

17. Explain what Flesch's book, "Why Johnny Can't Read," contributed to research on methods of teaching reading.

18. List several differences between good and poor readers.

19. Define dyslexia and attention deficit disorder, and relate what is known about the causes and treatment of each.

REVIEW EXERCISE--FILL IN THE BLANKS

1. The youngest children entering first grade are about _____ younger than the oldest ones. If a child is not ready for first grade, making her _____ is probably not as good an idea as enrolling her in a pre-first grade program. Also, _____ a poor student in a grade is not likely to improve performance.

2. _____, as measured by IQ scores, is one of the best predictors of school performance. If IQ scores fail to accurately predict school success, it is most likely in the case of a _____ (high/low) scoring child who does _____.

3. Two kinds of mental retardation are _____, due to brain defects, and _____, due to environmental deprivation. Most cases of retardation are due to _____. In terms of severity, most retarded children are in the _____ category.

4. Intellectually gifted children tend to be _____ (superior/ inferior) in most aspects of living.

5. Childrearing styles may contribute to the differences in school performance between black and white students. Black children seem to have less _____ in problem solving situations. Cultural differences are also apparent when comparing Asian children to American children. Asians seem to place greater emphasis on _____ and _____.

6. Girls do better in school when it comes to _____ and _____. Boys do better on _____ tasks. Learning disabilities are more commonly found among _____.

7. Among European and American children the _____ parenting style tends to produce higher school achievement. Children who grow up in one-parent families tend to do _____ (better/worse) in school than children with two parents.

8. The ability to come up with unusual solutions to problems and to think of unusual uses for common objects illustrates _____ thinking. This skill is important in _____.

9. Being rewarded for something from the outside is called _____ motivation. Being rewarded for something from the inside is called _____ motivation. If _____ does not exist, outside rewards might be useful, and eventually the reward may be _____.

10. For children with a _____-goal orientation, praise and grades are important motivators. Children with a _____-goal orientation are not as impressed with grades because they are learning for mastery, not for rewards.

11. Children who have doubts about their ability, and do not believe that ability is likely to change, tend not to attempt something unless they know they can _____. Those who believe that ability can be stretched by hard work tend to rise to a challenge and most often take a _____-goal orientation.

12. Three aspects of attribution for success or failure are _____, _____ and _____. People who believe they can control their own success and failure have an _____ locus of control. People who believe that other people or circumstances are the determining factors have an _____ locus of control.

13. Making things too easy for slow learners is probably a _____ idea. This tends to merely produce the _____ of intelligence.

14. Three marks of a successful school are an administration committed to _____, teachers who have high _____ for their students, and a _____ atmosphere.

15. One reason children from different cultures do not do equally well in school is that some cultures may have _____ that conflict with those of the school.

16. If a child does well in school because the teacher has a favorable opinion of her skills (justified or not), this would be an example of a _____.

17. "Counting on" is a technique where the child begins counting from a number other than _____. For a child to count on his fingers in the early stages of math learning is probably a _____ (good/bad) idea. It tends to _____ the likelihood of correct answers and allows the child to _____ math facts more easily.

18. Asian children may learn math more easily than English speakers because their _____ treats numbers in a more logical fashion.

19. Two major methods of teaching reading are the _____ technique and the use of _____. Users of _____ have a better ability to decode words they have not seen before and therefore seem to be at an advantage.

20. A poor reader who does well on other academic tasks may be _____. A child who cannot sit still and concentrate may have _____. Both of these problems are called learning _____. They both may be the result of _____.

PRACTICE EXAM

1. The main job or career of middle childhood is _____.
   A. playing
   B. going to school
   C. growing up physically
   D. choosing an occupation

2. Good performance in school _____.
   A. is typical of all famous scientists and celebrities
   B. is highly correlated with success in adult life
   C. is more a social expectation on the part of parents than a necessity in real life
   D. is almost always determined by genetic factors

3. One criterion for the diagnosis of mental retardation is an IQ score _____.
   A. below 100
   B. between 80 and 90
   C. below 70
   D. between 90 and 110

4. The correlation between IQ score and school performance is around _____.
   A.   .10   C.   .60
   B.   .50   D.   .80

5. IQ scores <u>perfectly</u> predict _____.
   A.   adult success
   B.   academic achievement
   C.   social skills
   D.   nothing

6. According to your textbook, as many as _____ percent of the American population is mentally retarded.
   A.   2   C.   7
   B.   5   D.   10

7. Biologically caused retardation is called _____.
   A.   psychoneural
   B.   cultural familial
   C.   endogenous
   D.   organic

8. Most mentally retarded children _____.
   A.   are in the mildly retarded category
   B.   are institutionalized
   C.   have organic problems
   D.   cannot be left unattended

9. In general, how do white children compare to black and Asian children in school performance?
   A.   worse in all respects
   B.   better in all respects
   C.   better than blacks but worse than Asians
   D.   better than Asians but worse than blacks

10. Your textbook reports that most of the differences between the school performances of various ethnic groups can be attributed to _____.
    A.   cultural and social factors
    B.   genetics
    C.   dietary differences
    D.   bilingual versus English-only speakers

11. Children with high IQs tend to be _____.
    A.   less aggressive
    B.   taller and healthier than other children
    C.   better adjusted psychologically
    D.   all of the above

12. The average boy does better than the average girl on IQ items _____.
    A.   overall
    B.   having to do with mathematics
    C.   having to do with verbal skills
    D.   having to do with reading

13. A disproportionate number of verbally handicapped students are _____.
    A. male
    B. female
    C. Asian
    D. overweight

14. In white and Hispanic families, a(n) _____ parenting style tends to produce the best school performance.
    A. authoritarian
    B. permissive
    C. institutional
    D. authoritative

15. Annie couldn't find a paper clip to hold her school report together. Which of the following alternatives is the best example of divergent thinking on her part?
    A. a staple
    B. a straight pin
    C. a happy face sticker
    D. folding over a corner

16. Reflectiveness and impulsiveness are examples of _____.
    A. internal and external locus of control
    B. attribution styles
    C. cognitive styles
    D. learning disabilities

17. When is the best time to depend on extrinsic motivation as opposed to intrinsic motivation?
    A. when intrinsic motivation is lacking altogether
    B. when the child is gifted
    C. when the child needs money
    D. when there is already a great deal of internalized motivation

18. Which of the following statements best typifies a learning-goal orientation toward school?
    A. The grade is the most important thing.
    A. If I fail, people will think I am stupid.
    C. I took that class because I love a challenge.
    D. I only like classes I know I can succeed in.

19. Three dimensions of attribution for success or failure are _____.
    A. id, ego and superego
    B. stability, global-ness, locus of control
    C. intrinsic, extrinsic and internalized rewards
    D. impulsivity, reflectivity, introspectiveness

20. Which of the following is the best example of an external locus of control?
    A.   All things come to him who waits.
    B.   He who hesitates is lost.
    C.   Seize the day!
    d.   Success is 1% inspiration and 99% perspiration.

21. Among other things, successful schools _____.
    A.   are not racially mixed
    B.   have more books in their libraries
    C.   have more teachers with advanced degrees
    D.   emphasize a safe and orderly environment

22. In moving away from the idea of a "melting pot" toward one that values cultural diversity, providing a good education becomes more difficult because _____.
    A.   more disadvantaged children are entering the schools
    B.   cultural diversity means the presence of conflicting values and attitudes toward education
    C.   every student must become bilingual
    D.   different schools must be provided for the varying genetic abilities of different ethnic groups

23. Which of the following is true of computers in the classroom?
    A.   Computers may widen the gap between achievements of boys and girls.
    B.   Computers may widen the gap between good and poor students
    C.   Computers tend to penalize children who do not know how to type.
    D.   All of the above

24. The self-fulfilling prophecy is _____.
    A.   mere superstition
    B.   when teachers give a student good grades after the student plays "teacher's pet"
    C.   an example of how belief about something can affect the way it actually turns out
    D.   a technique for teaching self-efficacy

25. Informal, open classrooms _____.
    A.   freed students from restrictive routines and resulted in more actual on-task time
    B.   tended to produce aimless, unstructured behavior on the part of students
    C.   are the latest approach to education based on the most recent research
    D.   demonstrated that Piaget was wrong about the order of stage development

26. Which of the following statements about the learning of
    mathematics is true?
    A. Finger counting may be beneficial to students in the
        early stages of learning math.
    B. Making a lot of mistakes increases learning speed,
        because the child learns what is wrong as well as
        what is right.
    C. Asian Americans usually do more poorly than blacks.
    D. By junior high, girls usually outscore the boys.

27. How are some Asian languages better at representing numbers
    than is English?
    A. They do not have a spoken form for numbers, only a
        written form.
    B. They have abandoned the Arabic system of representing
        numbers and replaced it with the Roman system.
    C. They speak number words in a more logical manner which
        conveys the meaning more effectively.
    D. Finger signs accompany the speaking of number words.

28. Many children who have trouble learning to read _____.
    A. don't scan the letters from left to right
    B. are less able to break words up into their separate
        sounds
    C. are also deficient in motor coordination skills
    D. nevertheless tend to be very good writers

29. An estimated _____ percent of American children are
    classified as being learning disabled.
    A. 10   C. 30
    B. 20   D. 50

30. Attention deficit disorder with hyperactivity (ADD-H)_____.
    A. is characterized by long periods of rocking and
        blank staring
    B. cannot usually be treated medically
    C. may involve hereditary factors
    D. is usually outgrown by high school

THOUGHT QUESTIONS

1. Do you remember ever having a special teacher like Miss A?
    If so, what was it about him/her that impressed you?

2. What is the difference between mental retardation and a
    learning disability?

3. While America is largely a nation of immigrants, two groups
    of immigrants, black Americans and Asian Americans, seem to
    represent opposite extremes as far as school achievement is
    concerned. Your text offers some explanations for this.
    Can you think of any others--ones that might be related to
    the different experiences these groups have had in coming
    to America?

ANSWERS WITH PAGE REFERENCES

Fill in the Blanks

1. one year (382)
    wait a year (383)
    retaining (383)
2. Intelligence (384)
    high (384)
    poorly (384)
3. organic (386)
    cultural-familial (386)
    cultural-familial (387)
    mild (387)
4. superior (385)
5. confidence (388)
    hard work (388)
    devotion to
       parents (388)
6. verbal skills (389)
    reading (389)
    visual-spatial (389)
    boys (389)
7. authoritative (391)
    worse (391)
8. divergent (392)
    creativity (392)
9. extrinsic (395)
    intrinsic (395)
    intrinsic (395)
    internalized (395)
10. performance (396)
    learning (396)

11. succeed (396)
    learning (396)
12. stability (397)
    global/specific (397)
    locus of control (398)
    internal (398)
    external (398)
13. bad (402)
    illusion (402)
14. academic excellence
       (401)
    expectations (401)
    safe, orderly (401)
15. values (402)
16. self-fulfilling
       prophecy (406)
17. one (407)
    good (408)
    increase (408)
    memorize (408)
18. language (409-410)
19. sight-reading (411)
    phonics (411)
    phonics (412)
20. dyslexic (415)
    attention deficit
       disorder with
       hyperactivity (416)
    disabilities (416)
    brain abnormality (416)

Multiple Choice

1.	B (382)	9.	C (386-88)	17.	A (395)	25.	B (395)
2.	B (382)	10.	A (386-88)	18.	C (396)	26.	A (408)
3.	C (387)	11.	D (385)	19.	B (397-98)	27.	C (410)
4.	C (384)	12.	B (389)	20.	A (398)	28.	B (413)
5.	D (384)	13.	A (389)	21.	D (401)	29.	A (416)
6.	A (387)	14.	D (391)	22.	B (402)	30.	C (417)
7.	D (386)	15.	C (392)	23.	D (405)		
8.	A (387)	16.	C (393)	24.	C (406)		

SUGGESTED ANSWERS TO THOUGHT QUESTIONS

1. If yes, compare the qualities you remember with those
    mentioned in the text.

2. Mental retardation involves a <u>general</u> lack of intellectual skills, <u>combined with</u> below average ability to adapt to the environment as a whole. A learning disability, on the other hand, is restricted to a fairly narrow aspect of intellectual functioning, such as reading or the ability to concentrate. Other abilities are largely unaffected.

3. Most blacks were originally brought to this country involuntarily, as slaves, having no control over their lives. This could quite naturally produce a pervasive "external" locus of control. Even after slavery, discriminatory behavior coming from the rest of the population could hardly help but be detrimental to their cultural and personal functioning. Many Asians, on the other hand, came here seeking a better life, often at great expense and danger to themselves. One might expect that people who would voluntarily undertake such an extreme dislocation would be among the most adventurous, highly motivated and "internal," as far as locus of control is concerned. Overcoming hardship and meeting challenges is already a big part of their lives. Carrying this attitude over into the classroom would naturally lead to academic success.

Chapter 13

Getting Along with Oneself
and with Others

AN OVERVIEW OF THE CHAPTER

Chapter Thirteen deals with the development of self-knowledge and the growth of interpersonal relationships in the school-age child. Social cognition, a form of metacognition in which one becomes aware of people's thoughts and feelings, begins to develop early in childhood. But it is not until the child is 8 or 9 years old that he can begin to distinguish genuine emotional messages from false ones, and it is several years more before he can convincingly conceal his own emotions from others.

Along with increasing awareness of emotional life comes the realization that people are more complex than outward appearance would lead one to believe. It often takes until late childhood for a child to realize that people do not always fit into neat stereotypes, and that each person can be described by a variety of internal qualities, some flattering and some not so flattering.

Self-perception also improves with time, and children become more realistic in evaluating their own academic, athletic and social abilities. Most children also boost and preserve their self-esteem by valuing and concentrating on their strengths to compensate for their weaknesses.

Sex-role concepts and stereotypes are acquired very early and by the late preschool years, very rigid stereotypes are in place. As children mature, however, this rigidity may be softened, especially if they are exposed to more androgynous role models. Children who are androgynous (who exhibit positive characteristics of both genders) are also likely to have high self-esteem, especially if the child is female.

Peer relationships among school-age children are typically same-sex relationships. The female group associations that develop during this period tend to be characterized by cooperative interaction, while male groups are characterized by

aggressive competition. In mixed groups, the boys tend to
dominate. Friendships among school children become more stable
with increasing age as the child begins to base relationships on
more enduring internal characteristics instead of transient
external ones. Friendships among girls tend to be more
exclusive than those found among boys, and may also be more
easily upset by feelings of jealousy.

     Children who are at particular risk for later problems are
those who are rejected (who are rated negatively by their peers)
and those who are neglected (who are ignored by their peers).
Rejected children, in particular, are more likely to engage in
long-term patterns of antisocial behavior unless the
circumstances that lead to their rejection are dealt with. Even
then, only about half of rejected children overcome their social
problems.

     The family environment is important in the development of
social relationships in children. Children tend to model what
they see, and form relationships similar to the ones they
experience themselves. Parental rules and values are more
likely to be followed by children if the parents communicate
these principles clearly and live by them themselves. Teaching
by induction (using reasoned arguments for or against a certain
behavior) is more effective than teaching by power-assertion
(the use of threats and punishment without explanations).

     The ability to put oneself in another's position is the
basis for moral awareness and altruistic behavior. There are
several stage-type theories of moral development, and most
recent research seems to support the position of Eisenberg, who
proposes six flexible stages of moral reasoning. While children
may progress through stages of moral development, going from
self-interested reasoning toward decisions based on internalized
general principles, there is also evidence that children (and
many adults) still have their ethical decision-making swayed
more by circumstances than by larger concepts of right and
wrong.

     The chapter also includes special sections on racial
prejudice among children and childhood antisocial behavior.

KEY TERMS AND CONCEPTS

social cognition   induction
androgynous   role-taking ability
rejected children   altruism
neglected children   antisocial behavior
power-assertive discipline

CHAPTER OBJECTIVES--CHECK YOURSELF
By the time you've finished reading and studying this chapter,
you should be able to:

  1. Define social cognition, and trace the development of this

skill in the preschool and school-age child.

2. Describe the changing ways children form opinions about other people as they grow older.

3. Describe the changes in behavior attribution that occur as the child matures.

4. Describe the development of gender stereotypes in children and the effects these have on behavior. Make reference to androgyny as an alternative to rigidly held gender roles.

5. Describe the styles of group interaction common among school-age boys and school-age girls.

6. Discuss how the different social interaction styles of boys and girls affect friendship patterns.

7. Discuss how friendship relationships vary with age and cognitive level.

8. Define rejected and neglected children, and discuss the causes of rejection and social neglect.

9. Summarize research on antisocial behavior in children and relate this problem to social neglect.

10. Summarize the influence of parental behavior and family environment on the social adjustment of the child.

11. Summarize research on power-assertive and inductive styles of discipline.

12. Discuss the relationship between social cognition, role-taking ability and altruism in children.

13. Summarize Eisenberg's theory of moral development and contrast it with the theory proposed by Kohlberg.

14. Discuss the relative impact of moral principles and environmental circumstance on moral decision-making in children.

REVIEW EXERCISE--FILL IN THE BLANKS

1. Knowledge and understanding of other people's thoughts and feelings and of how people interact is called _____. The ability to read emotions in someone else's face and get social information from those emotions is called _____.

2. Children begin to reliably detect the difference between genuine and pretended emotional expression in others by the age of _____. The ability to regulate _____ comes before

the ability to regulate facial expression of feelings. Children sometimes try to deal with strong emotions by trying to make them _____.

3. People tend to stereotype others. Children (as well as adults) often _____ information about others that does not fit the stereotype.

4. Methods of defining the self change as the child grows. Younger children tend to describe themselves in terms of _____ characteristics, while older children advance to describing themselves in terms of more _____ traits. The older child is also more willing to admit that not all of her characteristics are _____ ones.

5. Children (and adults as well) often attribute their own behavior, especially bad behavior, to _____ causes, while attributing the behavior of others to _____ causes.

6. Older school-age children manage to maintain and protect their self-esteem by emphasizing the things they are _____ at and de-emphasizing the things they are _____ at.

7. Sex-role stereotypes are often less rigid in _____ children than they are in _____ ones. Someone who demonstrates both masculine and feminine characteristics is said to be _____. These individuals tend to have a higher _____ than children who possess only _____ characteristics. This is probably because _____ characteristics are valued most highly in society.

8. Children in the school-age years tend to associate most exclusively with members of their own _____. Girls' groups are characterized by _____ and _____, whereas boys' groups are characterized by _____ and _____.

9. Interracial harmony is best achieved among children if they can get to know each other as _____.

10. In middle childhood, _____ influence the behavior of children more than their _____ do.

11. In middle childhood, fantasy games tend to be replaced by games with clear-cut _____. Younger children enjoy games characterized by role _____, and older children get more involved with games in which there are _____.

12. Friendships among young children tend to be based on more _____ factors than the friendships of older children. Friendships among girls tend to be _____, _____, and _____, while friendships among boys are more _____ and _____. Girls' friendships are _____ likely to be disrupted by jealousy.

13. Children who are neither liked nor disliked by their peers are called _____ children. They tend to be "invisible" in their peer group. Children who are actively disliked by their peers are called _____ children. Aggressive children in this last group are often at risk for social difficulties in later years, specifically _____ behavior.

14. Trouble at home can be disruptive to a child's social and emotional development. In a troubled family situation, the _____ is most likely to be emotionally distant from the children. In the typical family, _____ are not encouraged to be as open about feelings as are _____. Boys tend to be punished _____ than girls.

15. _____ discipline is based on threats and punishment. _____ discipline is based on reasoned explanations of the rules.

16. "Walking a mile in someone else's shoes" is an example of _____. If this leads to the person learning to experience the other individual's feelings, then the person is demonstrating _____. _____ is going out of your way to help someone else, even though there may be nothing in it for you.

17. Children who exhibit a chronic pattern of antisocial behavior are said to be _____.

18. _____ believes that Kohlberg's theory of moral reasoning is too rigid, and has proposed another theory of her own. While children may progress through stages of moral reasoning, there is evidence that the _____ may play a bigger role in honesty than moral principles do.

PRACTICE EXAM

1. Which of the following is a type of metacognition?
   A. gender typing
   B. social cognition
   C. induction
   D. decentering

2. Social referencing, the ability to gather information from others through behavior, facial expression, etc., seems to be present in children by the age of _____.
   A. one year
   B. three years
   C. six years
   D. nine years

3. A seven-year old child is asked to describe Santa Claus.
    Which of the following descriptions is most typical of that
    age?
    A. He is very generous and kind-hearted.
    B. He is big and fat and wears a red suit.
    C. He represents the spirit of giving.
    D. He likes all children but it makes him sad when they
        are bad.

4. Self-knowledge _____.
    A. develops more rapidly than knowledge about others
    B. reaches adult levels by the age of ten
    C. in children is limited to action-oriented behaviors,
        such as athletic performance
    D. may develop more slowly than knowledge of others

5. Younger children tend to attribute the behavior of other
    people to _____.
    A. stable, internal characteristics
    B. free will
    C. temporary, external causes
    D. fears and instincts

6. Children who are low on both typical male and typical
    female characteristics are termed _____.
    A. masculine
    B. feminine
    C. androgynous
    D. undifferentiated

7. Which of the following types of individual tends to have
    the highest self-esteem?
    A. masculine
    B. feminine
    C. androgynous
    D. both A and C about equally

8. School-age children segregate themselves most strictly
    according to _____.
    A. sex
    B. race
    C. intelligence
    D. socioeconomic status

9. Which of the following statements best represents "girl
    group" interaction style?
    A. I can do that better than you can.
    B. I was here first. You have to go behind me.
    C. How about this? I'll find the dog and you get the
        wagon.
    D. Bang! You're dead!

10. Which of the following attempts at getting children of different races to like each other is most likely to succeed?
   A. Put them in small groups, divide them into inter-racial pairs and have them solve problems together.
   B. Divide them into teams along racial lines and have them compete against each other.
   C. Make them live together in large groups.
   D. Separate them into racial groups and educate them about the good points of the other group.

11. If a relationship is reciprocal but has no underlying continuity, Selman would call it a _____ relationship.
   A. playmateship
   B. one-way assistance
   C. fair-weather cooperation
   D. intimate and mutually shared

12. Friendships of later childhood are more stable and last longer because _____.
   A. older children are more suspicious and choose their friends with great care
   B. younger children base friendships on more superficial and temporary factors
   C. older children make friends only with members of the same sex
   D. younger children are more conscious of racial differences

13. Friendships among girls are more troubled by _____ than friendships among boys.
   A. jealousy and exclusivity
   B. competitiveness
   C. lack of cooperation
   D. aggression

14. Children who are liked by some of their peers but disliked by others are called _____ children.
   A. popular
   B. rejected
   C. average
   D. controversial

15. Neglected children are those who _____.
   A. received mainly negative evaluations from others
   B. often go unnoticed by others
   C. get about the same number of positive ratings as popular children
   D. receive more negative ratings than rejected children

16. Rejected children may be the victims of a number of "vicious circles." This means that _____.
   A. their peers, their parents and their school teachers all dislike them and pick on them
   B. other children gang up on them and assault them
   C. poor social skills tend to run in families
   D. their behavior has undesirable consequences which, in turn, tend to produce more undesirable behavior

17. Trouble in the family has more of a harmful effect on younger children than on older ones. This is because _____.
   A. older children are less dependent on their parents
   B. older children are more likely to take personal responsibility for the problem and own up to it
   C. younger children are more likely to blame the parents
   D. younger children are more likely to be rejected children

18. In middle childhood, the most influential people in a child's life are likely to be _____.
   A. younger siblings
   B. parents
   C. same-sex peers
   D. opposite-sex peers

19. School-age girls are more likely to conform to parental demands than boys because _____.
   A. parents are more critical of girls' disobedience
   B. boys are greatly influenced by their girlfriends
   C. girls are not taught to be very independent compared to boys
   D. girls have a built-in desire to please their fathers stemming from the Electra Complex

20. Power assertive discipline _____.
   A. includes reasons and justifications
   B. uses threats and punishments
   C. most often results in internalized moral standards
   D. has little short-term effect on behavior

21. Luigi's father tells him not to scatter trash on the driveway because "it makes us look like messy people and it could also be dangerous." This is an example of _____.
   A. discipline based on induction
   B. an appeal to metacognitive skills
   C. permissive parenting
   D. power-assertive discipline

22. Parents should try to make the messages they send to their children as consistent and unambiguous as possible because _____.
    A. children try to get away with as much as they can
    B. children can interpret unclear or inconsistent messages in ways you may not intend
    C. children cannot understand long sentences
    D. children respond only to concrete commands and questions

23. "Just think of how I feel when you don't tell me where you are going." This parent is asking the child to engage in _____.
    A. altruistic behavior
    B. moral decision making
    C. role-taking behavior
    D. concrete operational thinking

24. Empathy is _____.
    A. feeling sorry for someone
    B. doing the right thing in an ethical dilemma
    C. imitating what you see someone else doing
    D. experiencing someone else's feelings

25. Which of the following is an example of altruistic behavior?
    A. trading favors with another child
    B. helping someone in hopes of getting recognition
    C. sharing your lunch with a child who could not afford one even when you are very hungry yourself
    D. giving another child your spinach because you were going to throw it away anyway

26. We can expect about _____ of school-age boys with antisocial behavior to improve as they mature.
    A. one fourth
    B. one half
    C. three fourths
    D. all

27. Whose theory of moral development argues that moral reasoning is universal and follows the same sequence of steps everywhere in the world?
    A. Piaget's
    B. Kohlberg's
    C. Eisenberg's
    D. Erikson's

28. Which stage in Eisenberg's approach to moral reasoning is characterized by issues of personal gain or loss?
    A. self-centered reasoning
    B. needs-oriented reasoning
    C. approval-oriented reasoning
    D. empathic reasoning

29. To make moral decisions on the basis of internalized principles means that _____.
   A. one is responding to rewards and punishments
   B. one has taken certain ideas of right and wrong to heart and made them one's own
   C. one is responding to the demands of authority
   D. the anticipation of reciprocal treatment is the prime motivator for good behavior

30. Probably the most influential factor in determining the degree of honesty in children is _____.
   A. the degree of religious commitment
   B. the situation
   C. the sex of the individual
   D. the effect of dishonest behavior on others

THOUGHT QUESTIONS

1. A father says that "A good whipping is what kids need to teach them right from wrong." According to research presented in your text, does such treatment really teach children right from wrong? If not, what does it teach them?

2. Do you think that racism could be eliminated if one or two generations of children could be brought up without exposure to adults modeling racist behavior and attitudes? Or would the kids re-invent the problem all over again on their own?

3. Why would an androgynous gender orientation improve the self-image of girls more than that of boys?

ANSWERS WITH PAGE REFERENCES

Fill in the Blanks

1. social cognition (422)
   social referencing (422)
2. 8 or 9 (423)
   verbal expression (423)
   go away (424)
3. disregard (425)
4. physical (426)
   psychological (426)
   good (426)
5. external (426)
   internal (426)
6. good (428)
   bad (428)

7. older (428)
   younger (428)
   androgynous (429)
   self-esteem (429)
   feminine (429)
   masculine (429)
8. sex (430)
   cooperation and
      avoidance of
      conflict (432)
   competition and
      dominance (432)
9. individuals (433)

10. peers (435)
    parents (435)
11. rules (435)
    reversal (435)
    winners and
       losers (435)
12. superficial (436)
    close, intimate
       and exclusive (438)
    competitive and
       aggressive (439)
    more (439)
13. neglected (440)
    rejected (440)
    criminal (441)

14. father (444)
    boys (445)
    girls (445)
    more (445)
15. Power-assertive (445-46)
    Inductive (446)
16. role taking (448)
    empathy (448)
    Altruism (448)
17. conduct-disordered (450)
18. Eisenberg (452)
    situation (453)

Multiple Choice

1.	B (422)	9.	C (432)	17.	A (444)	25.	C (448)
2.	A (422)	10.	A (433)	18.	C (435)	26.	B (451)
3.	B (425)	11.	C (437)	19.	C (445)	27.	B (452)
4.	D (425)	12.	B (436)	20.	B (445)	28.	A (453)
5.	C (426)	13.	A (439)	21.	A (446)	29.	B (453)
6.	D (429)	14.	D (440)	22.	B (446)	30.	B (453)
7.	D (429)	15.	B (440)	23.	C (448)		
8.	A (430)	16.	D (442)	24.	D (448)		

SUGGESTED ANSWERS TO THOUGHT QUESTIONS

1. Severe physical punishment probably does not teach the child any lasting lessons about "right and wrong." Such treatment would barely bring the child beyond the first stages of moral thinking as described by either Kohlberg or Eisenberg. On the other hand, this kind of discipline does teach that certain behaviors are punished, and that aggression is a suitable means for controlling the behavior of others. It probably also teaches the child that not getting caught is important if you intend to break the rules. A better approach might be the inductive method, in which the parent leads and coaches the child in ethical behavior. The internalization of values is more likely to occur in this case.

2. From a variety of evidence presented in the text, it appears that children are very good at noticing differences between themselves and other children and then evaluating those differences in a negative way (see the sections on opposite-sex avoidance and rejected children, for example). Vicious circles of alienation seem to follow, leading to greater dislike. Could it be that the hormone-induced attraction to the opposite sex that occurs in puberty is all that prevents sex-discrimination from taking on the

more extreme proportions of racism? Of course, such tendencies to avoid and dislike the "outsider" may have had some survival value long ago when life was more vicious and chancy. But now, we stand to gain much more by modifying such tendencies and learning more tolerant responses. It may be, however, that each generation will have to learn tolerance on its own.

3. Self-image is at least in part based on society's evaluation of you and your characteristics, and society seems to value masculine traits more highly than feminine traits. Since androgynous individuals share both masculine and feminine traits, this means that boys would not be losing highly valued traits in becoming androgynous, but girls would be gaining them. Thus, girls would be expected to benefit more in the area of self-esteem.